30 WAYS TO BE FAMOUS
AFTER RETIREMENT

PHILIPPE ANDRES

30 WAYS TO BE FAMOUS AFTER RETIREMENT

SUMMARY

I. Prologue

II. OK Boomers Are Not Yogurts

III. 30 Ways to Be Famous After Retirement

1. Already Famous and Knowing How to Stay That Way: Clint Eastwood, Brigitte Bardot, Mick Jagger, Henry Salvador, Paul McCartney, Dolly Parton.
2. Revealing Yourself Late: Louise Bourgeois, Hokusai, Yayoi Kusama, the Popes.
3. Engaging in Extreme Sports or Achieving Sporting Feats: Rut Larsson, Yuichiro Miura, Fauja Singh, Olga Kotelko, Julia Welles Hawkins.
4. Making Discoveries: Pierre Agostini, Luc Montagnier, Vernon Lomax Smith, Louis Pasteur, Peter Higgs.
5. Going to Space: John Goodwin, Wally Funk.
6. Influencing on Social Media: Studio Danielle, Shirley Curry, Baddie Winkle.

7. Doing Radio/Television or Advertising: Mère Denis, Walter Bingham, Madame Soleil.

8. Becoming an Academician or Receiving a Literary Prize: Annie Ernaux, Marguerite Yourcenar, Katherine Anne Porter

9. Becoming the Hero of a Crisis or Entrepreneurial Saga: Harland David Sanders, Eric Raoult, Didier Lombard, Warren Buffett.

10. Turning to Crime: Harvey Weinstein, Bernard Madoff, Gaston Dominici.

11. Becoming Head of State: Deng Xiaoping, Leonid Brezhnev, Joe Biden, Nelson Mandela, Golda Meir, François Hollande, François Mitterrand.

12. Time Traveling: The Count of Saint Germain, Baba Vanga, Philippe Aries, Jean de Joinville.

13. Surviving War, Disaster, or Great Human Adventure: Claude Bloch, Leon Gautier (Commando Kieffer), Sunao Tsuboi, Millvina Dean, Lazare Ponticelli, Carlos Soria Fontan.

14. Having a Big Mouth, Oratory Talent, Being Scary: Georges Clemenceau, Jean Luc Melenchon, Jean Marie Le Pen, Donald Trump.

15. Defying Natural Laws: Paul Richard Alexander, Charlie Bancarel, James Hiram Bedford, Jean-Pierre Adams, Cornelia Ras.

16. Becoming a Great War Chief: Philippe Pétain, Paul Von Hindenburg, Cochise.

17. Philosophizing, Doing Sociology or Psychoanalyzing: Sigmund Freud, Edgar Morin, Arthur Schopenhauer.

18. Creating Fashion, Doing Photography: Jacques Henri Lartigue, Iris Apfel, Rose Victoria Repetto.

19. Becoming an Actor, Producer, Filmmaker, Costumer: Judi Dench, Youn Yuh-Jung, Ridley Scott, Ann Roth.

20. Having Children, Building a Family: Al Pacino, Robert De Niro, Omkari Panwar, Ramjit Raghav, Anthony Quinn.

21. Seduction and Courting: Massimo Gargia, Ninon de Lenclos, Zsa Zsa Gabor

22. Loving Sex: Richard Allan, Shigeo Tokuda, Dodo La Saumure, Dennis Hof.

23. Prophesying, Doing Good: Sister Emmanuelle, Mother Teresa, Moses, Gandhi

24. Blowing Out Candles: Jeanne Calment, Jiroemon Kimura.

25. Breaking the Bank: Théodore Struyck, Gloria McKenzie, Dennis Banfield.

26. Playing Solitaire: Sir Francis Chichester, Alejandra Ródriguez.

27. Being Intimate with a Celebrity: René Angeli, Thomas Markle, Jamie Spears, Mohamed Al-Fayed.

28. Becoming Famous After Death: Paul Cezanne, Paul Gauguin, Saint Thérèse of Lisieux.

29. Staging Yourself: Henri Charrière, Jacques Mayol.

30. Writing a Book on How to Become Famous After 70 or Finding the Thirty-First Way

PROLOGUE

PROLOGUE

I dedicate this book to my son Adrien, 16 and a half years old, who, without my knowledge, practiced urban exploration (or Urbex) in New York City. He put his life at risk, at the top of towers, suspension bridges, and cranes that he climbed without any safety measures for the thrill of a successful selfie immediately posted on social networks, following in the footsteps of one of his French idols, Alain Robert, who recently climbed the Total Energie tower in Paris-La Défense. Arrested several times by the New York Police Department (NYPD), notably for climbing a 1050-feet tower, my son is emblematic of other teenagers in major American or European cities who, in the hope of gaining instant fame on social networks, do not hesitate to put their lives in danger. TikTok or Instagram are full of such videos that garner tens of thousands of followers and even more likes. Adrien thus obtained 500,000 likes in two days following one of his videos where he appears at the top of a crane overlooking a tower. Belonging to the generation that was 16 years old in 1968, I do not recall risking our lives in any way for such an adrenaline rush or for a fleeting and short-lived quest for fame. It is true that social networks did not exist at that time and one could scandalize or stand out just by having long hair or wearing a miniskirt. From then on, I came up with the idea of reflecting on this quest for celebrity from a very young age at any cost and on this trend of *"looking good and avoiding looking bad"* which distorts true personalities and plunges us into the world of "fake", perception, virtual, and unreal. And then I discovered that more often than I thought, true fame could come later, even much later, for good or bad reasons, and that there was no point in rushing at 16 for this. Sometimes life, talent, work, perseverance, or even vice could open the doors to fame, well after the legal retirement age. I also discovered that older people still have extraordinary resources that lead them to accomplish incredible feats that one would think reserved for much younger individuals and which should make many generational conflicts seem ridiculous. This book goes against ageism and youthfulness. It is a tribute to the incredible qualities of human beings, where age is certainly a biological factor that affects the body, but certainly not the spirit.

OK BOOMERS ARE NOT YOGHURTS

OK BOOMERS ARE NOT YOGURTS

What's the worst thing for an *OK boomer* ? Becoming a *KO boomer* ! Wake up, OK boomers, and show that you still have what it takes! This book is for you and also for the younger generation because one day, you too will be nicknamed *OK millennial* or *OK Gen Z*. Being young is not just a privilege. As Paul Nizan, a French philosopher and writer who died in combat in 1940 at the age of 35, wrote: *"I was twenty. I will not let anyone say it's the best age of life."* In 1975, Romain Gary wrote a book titled *"Your Ticket Is No Longer Valid Beyond This Limit."* It's the story of a wealthy industrialist who, in his sixties, struggles to satisfy his young mistress sexually. This fear of sexual decline overwhelms him and gradually destroys his self-confidence and self-esteem. In this book, we will see that yes, your ticket remains valid until the grave, including sexually for some of us. As long as there is life, there is hope ! This biblical adage (Ecclesiastes 9.4) can also be turned into: "As long as there is hope, there is life", because hope is synonymous with life, "hope keeps you alive." This is why the desperate ones commit suicide! The hope of being recognized, or even famous, can be a powerful driving force in life and should not fade with age. One thing is certain: if we have no longer hope for anything, then what's the point of going from 70 to 80, then from 80 to 90, and beyond? And the hope of a life in the hereafter should not kill all hope here on earth! As the philosopher Roger-Pol Droit admirably writes, *growing old is not starting to die.*" In short, human beings are not yogurts with an expiration date, as excellently stated by Amanda Lear, muse of the later years of Salvador Dali. Human beings are like honey, imperishable until their death, even if it seems paradoxical, because ultimately aging is anything but a disease. Recently, the French philosopher André Comte-Sponville, who is 72 years old, declared in an interview with the newspaper Le Monde: *"Death can only take away a part of my old age, and probably not the most interesting part."* This is of course a very pertinent remark, which I will not dismiss out of hand, since I am the same age as him. However, I invite him to read this book, which may convince him that this reflection does not apply to everyone. In the United States, we now talk about Super Agers when referring to people over 80 who still have exceptional memory or at least as good as that of people 20 or 30 years younger. In this regard, let's mention the case of Akira Haraguchi, a Japanese engineer born in 1945, who in 2006, at the age of 61, managed to recite 100,000 digits of the number pi without making a mistake, for 16 hours. Certainly, fame is just one hope among others, but it is still incredibly motivating because it becomes more difficult to achieve with age ! So it's an interesting challenge to take on ! People over 70 represent about 15% of the population, at least in France or the United States. If they are not already famous, they should first know that according to various sources, there are generally fewer than 10 people out of

100,000 who are or become famous, regardless of age. Fame is a bit like the lottery. Anyone can try, but very few win! Some acquire it very young, even as babies, like the first test-tube baby, Amandine, Justin Bieber, or Demi Lovato, while others become famous Some achieve fame later in life, such as the naturalist and paleontologist Charles Darwin or the sculptor Louise Bourgeois, whose fame was truly acquired only after the age of 50. Others will only know posthumous fame, such as Amadeom Modigliani, an artist cursed during his lifetime, whose nudes have fetched over $150 million at auctions at Sotheby's or Christie's in New York. Regardless, this book will delight all those who would like to become famous, even if just for a single day, and who believe that it's never too late to achieve it. As Alain Robert, the French Spiderman who still climbs solo the cliffs of Verdon, in the south of France, at over 60 years old, says, *"the end of life is when we die, and until then, we can still do a lot of things; age is not an obstacle."* And whether one is already retired or still active, attempting to become famous past the age of sixty is a challenge much more fun than winning yet another game of Scrabble, golf, or bridge. Isn't it? This book lists around thirty ways to achieve fame, some more commendable than others, or downright unusual, but let's move past the means if the end goal is to become famous no matter what.

WAY NUMBER ONE

WAY NUMBER ONE : ALREADY BE FAMOUS AND KNOW HOW TO STAY FAMOUS.

At first glance, this method seems the easiest to achieve since one has already gained fame before the fateful retirement age and just needs to maintain it and live off the proceeds. However, considering the number of one-day or one-year stars who have now completely disappeared into oblivion, it seems easier said than done! The main reason is that you need to have talent and not just give the impression of having it! Of course, there are icons who will remain famous forever, regardless of their age and activity, and even after their death. Among the deceased, we can mention Neil Armstrong, Marilyn Monroe, Albert Einstein, Queen Elizabeth II, John F. Kennedy, Martin Luther King Jr., Charles de Gaulle, Mozart, Pablo Picasso, Andy Warhol, Karl Lagerfeld, or Pelé, and among the living, Brigitte Bardot, J.K. Rowling, Barack Obama, Mick Jagger, Elton John, Greta Thunberg, or Paul McCartney.

Why have these individuals become icons whose fame cannot be taken away from them? Undoubtedly because beyond their talents and achievements, they embody an era, an epic, strong trends, old or new values, revolutionary ideas, aspirations of an entire society for civil rights, freedom, equality, and non-discrimination. French actress Brigitte Bardot became the symbol of the free woman and advocate for animal rights. Just as Martin Luther King became the defender of civil rights for African Americans in the United States. Being part of history because one has shaped history is obviously the prerogative of politicians, and even more so of dictators or kings. From Julius Caesar to Mao Zedong, through Louis XIV, Napoleon Bonaparte, Adolf Hitler, Joseph Stalin, these different figures will remain in all memories, for their crimes or for their thirst for conquests and absolute power. Others, such as Mahatma Gandhi, John F. Kennedy, Nelson Mandela, Charles de Gaulle, or Leopold Sédar Senghor, are recognized for having been guides, inspired leaders, or examples to follow. Outside of politics, some will remain famous beyond their death because they have changed the lives of millions of people. We can mention Steve Jobs, the founder of Apple, who certainly changed our lifestyles more than any politician claiming to do so. This is also the case with The Beatles, whose influence on the history of rock is paramount, or Louis Pasteur, a pioneer in microbiology, whose efforts in the field of vaccination have saved countless lives and who invented the rabies vaccine at the age of 63. In his case, it's interesting to note that he even left for posterity a deformation of his name in a preservation process, pasteurization. Jesse Owens, the first black athlete to achieve international fame and multiple world champion in disciplines such as the 100m, 200m, 4x100m relay, and long jump, remains forever famous for winning four Olympic medals at the 1936 Olympics in Berlin, in front of Adolf Hitler, demolishing the myth of the superiority of "Aryans" over other races and thus contributing to the cause of African Americans in his own country, the United States. Sean Connery has become as legendary as James Bond himself, so much so that he personified the character to such an extent that he is recognized as the best of the six actors who have played the role. Sometimes one might even wonder if it wasn't James Bond who played the role of Sean Connery! The case of people who have acquired a certain level of fame in the past and succeed in maintaining it is often due to the fact that they do not stop working, producing, living, and loving well beyond the retirement age, to the point of becoming symbols for it. In French politics, this is true for former Presidents of the Fifth Republic who are still active in political life, as well as for some of their former Prime Ministers who have made the same choice. But who still remembers Jean-Marc Ayrault, the short-lived Prime Minister of François Hollande, not to mention the slew of ministers, all more or less fallen into deep obscurity, sometimes from the moment of their appointment ? In the United States, who can name the former Vice Presidents of George W. Bush, Barack Obama, or Donald Trump? Probably not many, and yet many of them are still alive but perhaps lacked the talent to remain in the spotlight. This is also true in the world of showbiz. If Madonna (65 years old) will remain famous until her death and even beyond, just like Elton John (76 years old), Mick Jagger (80 years old), or Paul MC-Cartney (81 years old), it's because they don't give up, just like the French singer Henri Salvador, who gave his last concert at the age of 90, or Dolly Parton. On the other hand, who still remembers the French singer Antoine, whose famous song "Élucubrations" marked his only success in 1966 and brought him fleeting fame? The same goes for the English singer Petula Clark, who is 90 years old today, and who enjoyed great international success during the sixties. Let's also mention the case of director and screenwriter Ridley Scott, who has just directed the excellent film

Napoleon at the age of 86. Certainly, Ridley Scott gained international renown with his famous science-fiction and horror film Alien, released in 1979 when he was just 42 years old, and he further solidified his reputation over time with cinematic successes such as Blade Runner in 1982, Thelma & Louise in 1991, Gladiator in 2000, Prometheus in 2012, not to mention the countless Alien sequels. But directing and producing Napoleon at 86 years old is still a remarkable display of vitality, creativity, and youthful spirit. So, when one becomes famous, if they want to remain so throughout their life and even beyond, there are three possible options :

1. **Become a symbol forever**, like James Dean, who died at 24, becoming a symbol of lost youth in Rebel Without a Cause and famously said, *"Dream as if you'll live forever, live as if you'll die today."* The same goes for the King, Elvis Presley, forever the undisputed master of rock and roll, or Marilyn Monroe, whose beauty combined with scandalous affairs with the Kennedys and tragic death at 36 from a barbiturate overdose make her a mythical actress of Hollywood's golden age. Often, a tragic and early end fuels the myth, as with Lady Diana, whose romantic misadventures and court struggles with the Windsors, as well as her fight against landmines, had already propelled her international fame to the highest level. Let's also mention the case of the French singer Claude François, electrocuted at 39 in his bathroom at the height of his glory. Claude François, known as "Clo-Clo," became a symbol of French variety in the 1970s. He sold over 70 million records, half of them after his death.

2. **Never stop producing, creating, or doing something for the common good.** Besides the aforementioned examples, Bernadette Chirac remains famous for her "yellow

coins" initiative even though her husband Jacques Chirac, ex president of France, is no longer alive. As for the comedian Coluche, who tragically died at 41 in a road accident, his posthumous fame today is more due to the generous action he initiated in favor of the less fortunate with the Restaurants du Coeur than to the precise memory of his humorous sketches or films. Let's also mention the sociologist and philosopher Edgar Morin, who continues to publish and express himself at 102. Alfred Nobel, the inventor of dynamite, an invention that allowed him to amass a great fortune, wrote a year before his death the testament by which the Nobel Prize would reward benefactors of humanity each year in various fields.

3.   **To be recognized only after one's death.** It's frustrating and no consolation for the person concerned, much less for their heirs, and of course, not so common. Besides the case of Amadeo Modigliani, the list of artists who only achieved fame after their death is quite extensive. Let's mention Vincent Van Gogh, whose works were ignored during his lifetime even though he was an undisputed master of color, notably with his famous Sunflowers painted in 1888. Interned at the asylum of Saint-Rémy-de-Provence after cutting off his ear following a dispute with Paul Gauguin in Arles, he moved to Auvers-sur-Oise, where he painted the church in 1890. After his supposed suicide in 1890, his legacy was secured thanks to the efforts of his brother Theo's widow, Johanna Bonger. Paul Gauguin also experienced a similar fate. While he referred to himself as a "talented Sunday painter," he struggled with his art even though he was part of the Impressionist group, which included his friends Pissarro and Degas. After his stays in Pont-Aven, he died in 1903 during his second trip to Tahiti. Gauguin did not sell any paintings at the Impressionists' ex-

hibition at the 1889 World's Fair. He died of a heart attack in 1903, largely unknown and plagued by depression, illness, and alcohol. Yet, one of his paintings done in Tahiti in 1882 sold for over 260 million euros in 2015! Being a cursed artist was also, and more recently, the fate of Jean-Michel Basquiat, who died at the age of 27 from a speedball overdose, a mixture of heroin and cocaine. Quickly noticed by prominent New York gallery owners, Basquiat achieved fame at the age of 21. The use of pictograms, such as the three-pointed crown or the crown of thorns, diverse and varied supports, slogans, set him apart, and his friendship and collaboration with Andy Warhol, as well as Madonna, forever established him as a symbol of pop culture.

WAY NUMBER TWO

WAY NUMBER TWO : REVEALING ONESELF LATE

" In well-born souls, valor does not wait for the number of years," declares Rodrigue in Le Cid. While it is true that many talents or innate gifts reveal themselves at a very young age, there are also others that only blossom much later, either because we did not have the opportunity to develop or showcase them, or simply because we were not even aware of having them. **Agatha Christie** wrote: *"Live today as if it were the last day. And make plans as if you were here for eternity."* In accordance with this adage, I invite all those who think they have received no gift or talent to discover them and to invest themselves even very late in a project that motivates them.

Louise Bourgeois, a sculptor famous for her giant spiders, her paintings of women-houses, and her phallic sculptures, was born in Paris in December 1911 into a family of weavers. Initially drawn to drawing, and animated both by hatred towards her adulterous father and love towards her mother humiliated by this situation, Louise Bourgeois abandoned her pencils and brushes in the early 1950s in New York, where she now resided with her American husband Robert Goldwater, to sculpt a number of totemic forms in wood. Her first exhibition in New York took place at the Peridot Gallery in 1949 when she was 38 years old. Abandoning wood and vertical structures in the early 1960s, Louise Bourgeois used plaster and latex, representing increasingly sexualized forms, often resembling a penis or a vulva, such as her series of sculptures entitled Janus. She then went to Italy in the 1960s to work with marble. During the years 1960 to 1982, she was very involved with young female artists who participated in militant exhibitions of feminist art organized by the Women's Liberation Movement (MLF). At the age of 62, she began teaching at the Pratt Institute, Cooper Union, and the New York Studio School while participating in the Whitney Biennial. In the 1970s, she changed the way she dealt with her favorite themes around sexuality, femininity, the body, and loneliness, and created monumental sculptures including the famous "spiders" that represent her mother (Maman 1999). In 1999, she received the Golden Lion at the Venice Biennale for her entire body of work. It was only at the age of 71 that she achieved real recognition during the first retrospective organized for a female artist at the MOMA in New York in 1982. Even later, in 2008, The Centre Pompidou museum in Paris presented an exhibition of over 200 works (paintings, sculptures, drawings, engravings) in collaboration with the Tate Modern in London. Subsequently, there were exhibitions at The Antoni Tàpies Foundation in Barcelona, followed by a complete exhibition of her series of cells "Structures of Existence: The Cells" at the Guggenheim Museum in Bilbao. In 2009, at the age of 98, she was honored by the National Women's Hall of Fame with nine other American citizens for having left a mark on the history of the United States.

Katsushika Hokusai was born in October 1760 in the Edo district near Tokyo, Japan. He spent his entire life there. At the age of three, he was adopted by a family of mirror makers, and at the age of 15, he began an apprenticeship within a workshop that produced woodblock prints, which was a very popular printing method in Japan during the 18th century. This technique is known as Ukiyo-e and allows for the creation of colorful paintings using woodblock prints. He completed this apprenticeship at the age of 18 by joining a printmaking school, the Katsukawa Shunsho Art School, named after his teacher Shunsho. Shunsho himself was a recognized artist of Ukiyo-e, which literally means "pictures of the floating world." Hokusai signed his early prints under the name Shunr.. Later, he expanded his artistic knowledge under another master, Yusen, from the Kano School of Arts. In 1793, he was expelled from Shunsho shortly after his master's death for reasons unknown. In the following years, he associated with circles of poets and Kabuki theater actors and illustrated some of their works under a new artist name, Sōri. Later, Hokusai would be known under more than thirty different names, which was a common practice at the time within the Japanese artistic community. Hokusai married twice, but both wives passed away shortly thereafter. However, he had five children with them, two boys and three girls, the youngest of whom also became an artist. Over time, Hokusai's work evolved from drawings of actors or courtiers to natural landscapes and representations of everyday life. It was in 1800 that his artist name became known in his social environment as Katsushika Hokusai. In 1814, he published a collection of sketchbooks, the Hokusai manga. In the following ten years, Hokusai's work gained popularity and recognition, but it was truly from the 1820s and 1830s, when Hokusai, having then surpassed sixty, that he reached the pinnacle of his art. During this period, he created one of his major works, the Thirty-Six

Views of Mount Fuji, including the famous Great Wave off Kanagawa. He notably used Prussian blue, a newly introduced color in Japan. Other series of paintings and prints followed, including Views of Famous Bridges, Waterfalls of Various Provinces, and series of Birds and Flowers, Large Flowers, and Small Flowers. From 1834 to 1849, he revisited the theme of Mount Fuji and published One Hundred Views of Mount Fuji. However, from 1839, following the fire in his studio, his star began to fade somewhat, notably due to competition from young artists. Nevertheless, nothing stopped Hokusai, who continued to paint at over 87 years old. He died in April 1849, at the age of 89, and reportedly said on his deathbed, *"If only Heaven would give me ten more years, even just five more years, then I could become a true painter."* One of his writings found after his death even indicates that he believed that it was only by reaching the age of 130 that he would truly reach the pinnacle of his pictorial art, having completely understood the essence of his subjects, whether birds, insects, plants, or fish. International recognition of Hokusai's talent came at the end of the 19th century, a period during which his work strongly influenced Impressionist painters such as Monet, Van Gogh, and Degas, as well as musicians like Claude Debussy, who incorporated the Great Wave off Kanagawa into his musical work La Mer.

Yayoi Kusama shares at least two common points with Louise Bourgeois. One is having developed a particular perception of sexuality following her father's adulterous affairs, and the other is late recognition. Yayoi Kusama was born in 1929 in Japan, and from the age of 10, she suffered from hallucinatory troubles from which she escaped through drawing and representing dots. She declares, *"My life is a dot lost among thousands of other dots,"* revealing her obsession with this motif since childhood. Her mother, seeking revenge for her husband's infidelities, tries to thwart her desire to pursue artistic studies and attempts to marry her off at any cost. This results in a new obsession with the representation of phallic symbols on her mind, already prone to childhood hallucinations. The Japanese society of the time, still very patriarchal, did not facilitate the emancipation and desire for independence of women. The hierarchical rules and traditional teaching methods of the Kyoto High School where she studied painting did not suit her at all. In the 1960s, settled in New York, she integrated into the hippie movement and advocated hostility towards war, established order, and embraced free love. Through her friendship with the female artist Georgia O'Keefe, she obtained exhibitions that allowed her to sell her works. Meeting notable figures such as Andy Warhol and Claes Oldenburg, she gradually became a prominent figure in the New York art scene. During these years, she notably painted her series of Infinity Nets. Her fear of sex and intimate relationships also led her to produce the Accumulation series, composed of numerous phallic pieces. This series was followed by the Infinity Mirror Room based on endless repetitions. In 1966, she caused a mini-scandal at the Venice Biennale where, although not invited, she installed 1500 reflective stainless steel balls on the lawn where the event took place, with a sign reading "Your Narcissism For Sale." Despite being expelled from the Biennale by the police, she captured the attention of visitors and understood that communication and publicity are essential elements for an artist's recognition. In the late 1960s, she caused another mini-scandal on Wall Street by painting nude dancers with blue dots. Once again, the police intervened and stopped the happening. She resumed shortly after at the MOMA in New York by re-summoning her nude dancers for a performance titled Grand Orgy to Awaken the Dead, once again attracting attention to herself. In 1972, following the death of the assemblage artist Joseph Cornell, to whom she was very close, she worked on collages in homage to his memory. At that time, she returned to Japan and entered a psychiatric institution, wrote poetry, fiction, and produced artworks. Over the following period until 1993, her art remains relatively unknown until she is asked to represent Japan at the 45th Venice Biennale. Representing dotted pumpkins, one of her Infinity Mirror Room series achieves great success. Yayoi Kusama only gains international recognition starting from 1990, when she is already in her sixties. Today, Yayoi Kusama enjoys great international recognition by selling her works on all continents. In 2018, she was even ranked as the most expensive artist in the global art market. In Japan, the Yayoi Kusama museum is one of the most visited. Recently, a collaboration has been established between the Japanese artist and Louis Vuitton (LVMH), involving over 450 products of the prestigious luxury brand. Yayoi Kusama's portrait is now displayed on prestigious facades in Paris, London, New York, Milan, and Tokyo.

Being elected pope is another way to achieve international fame late in life. Indeed, if aside from insiders almost no one can name all the names of the approximately 130 eligible cardinals, the one among them who is elected pope by the 120 elector cardinals who compose the Conclave becomes famous worldwide on the very day of his election. Most popes are well into their sixties at the time of their election and in their eighties at the end of their pontificate. **Jorge Mario Bergoglio**, the current Pope Francis, former Archbishop of Buenos Aires, was elected to the papacy in 2013 at the age of 76 and is currently 87 years old. At the election, the pope becomes the Bishop of Rome, the head of the Catholic Church, and the monarchic head of state of the Vatican City. He thus becomes the natural interlocutor of all other heads of state abroad. While being elected pope is an indisputable way to achieve late international fame, it is not easy to be elected, even though the eligibility conditions are relatively broad: one must be a man, not be older than 80, and be baptized. The reality is, of course, more complicated since in practice, only about forty cardinals are "papabile" and eligible. That means being able to collect two-thirds of the votes of the Conclave. Pope Francis is appointed auxiliary bishop of Buenos Aires in 1992 and cardinal in 2001 by John Paul II. Before his election, he is already very popular in Argentina.

WAY NUMBER THREE

WAY NUMBER THREE : PRACTICING EXTREME SPORTS OR ACHIEVING SPORTS FEATS

In May 2022, **Rut Larsson,** a 103-year-old Swede, becomes the oldest person in the world to skydive. She immediately entered the Guinness World Records, of course. Rut said upon landing, *"It was wonderful to do this and I had been thinking about it for a long time."* Her helpers assisted her in getting up and handed her her walker. She rewarded herself for her own feat by eating a small cake. Her example has sparked enthusiasm on social media because by achieving her feat, Rut Larsson took the record from an American woman 78 days her junior, demonstrating that there is no age limit to fulfilling one's wildest dreams.

Yūichirō Miura, a Japanese mountaineer, became the oldest person to reach the summit of Everest in 2003 at the age of 70, a feat he repeated in 2008 at the age of 75 and in 2013 at 80. During his 2008 attempt, the record was temporarily taken from him by

Nepalese mountaineer **Min Bahadur Sherchan**, who achieved the same feat at the age of 76. It is worth noting that in 1970, Yūichirō Miura skied down the south col of Everest from 8,000 meters. He reached a speed of 150 km/h, his parachute intended to act as a brake proved useless, and he ended his uncontrolled descent just 100 meters from a huge crevasse. One day he declared: *"Everyone, regardless of age, should have a goal to achieve. It doesn't matter if it's big or small. It just has to be something you really want to do."* For him, if you have a dream to fulfill, you should never give up, because then dreams become reality. On his 90th birthday, he celebrated the event at the summit of Mount Teine in Sapporo at a much more modest altitude of 3,300 feet. His own father climbed Mount Kilimanjaro (19,340 feet) at the age of 77.

Fauja Singh, born in 1911 in India, participated in his first marathon at the age of 89, notably after losing one of his sons, who was decapitated by a metal sheet during a monsoon storm. Consumed by grief after this tragedy, he went to London to join another of his sons and began running to forget this drama. At the age of 90, he was already the fastest marathon runner in his category, completing the 26 miles in seven hours and 52 minutes. His last competitive race was a 6.2 miles course through Hong Kong, completed in an hour and a half at the age of 102. Fauja Singh's sporting activity brought him worldwide fame in the world of sports competitions, to the point that Adidas made him one of its spokespeople. He was a fragile child, and it was said that he only learned to walk at the age of 5.

There are also older and famous marathon runners, such as **Harriette Thompson**, who in 2015 at the age of 92 became the oldest woman to complete a marathon in San Diego. As a cancer survivor, her San Diego marathon raised over $100,000 for a charity funding research on leukemia and lymphoid diseases.

Olga Kotelko turned to athletics at the age of 77 with the help of a Hungarian coach. She then combined daily push-ups and intensive abdominal workouts. She added aqua aerobics sessions, breathing exercises, reflexology, and of course, athletics training. She participated in numerous Olympic-style sports events, including shot put, javelin, long jump, high jump, and various running events. What made her story particularly exceptional was her ability to set world records and perform at an undeniable level in her age group, frequently breaking records that stood for years. Her longevity and unusual athletic performances attracted the attention of researchers and scientists eager to understand the physiological and hereditary factors that contributed to her prosperity. Her support in various examinations shed light on the maturation system and the ability to monitor real health and well-being levels at a more advanced age. Olga Kotelko's story has motivated many people to stay active and pursue their interests regardless of aging. She remains the epitome of what can be achieved through confidence, dedication, and love for sports, even in the later stages of life.

Julia Welles Hawkins was born in February 1916 in Wisconsin, USA. After studying at Louisiana State University in Baton Rouge, she married Murray Hawkins in December 1941, just after the bombing of Pearl Harbor where Murray was stationed. The couple had four children, one of whom, their daughter Margaret, wrote a memoir about her mother. Known for her outstanding achievements in athletics, Julia "Hurricane" Hawkins began participating in track and field events at a very young age, quickly gaining attention and making waves in the sports world. At the age of 101, Hawkins ran the 100 meters in 40.12 seconds at the USATF Masters Outdoor Championships in 2017, becoming the oldest woman ever to achieve such a performance. She had run the 100 meters in 39.62 seconds earlier that year. Julia Hawkins also holds the record for the 60-meter sprint. Due to her remarkable speed despite her advanced age, this feat earned her the nickname "Hurricane Hawkins." She and Orville Rogers, aged 100, set world records for the 60-meter sprint at the USATF Masters Indoor Championships in 2018. Hawkins competed in sprints at the National Senior Games in June 2019. On August 15, 2021, **Diane "Flash" Friedman,** aged 100, beat Hawkins in the 100-meter race in her age group at the World Masters Games.

WAY NUMBER FOUR

WAY NUMBER FOUR : MAKING DISCOVERIES

Scientific research, of course, requires researchers to have both solid prior knowledge and excellent observational skills. They must also be creative and have a curiosity that allows them to break away from conventional thought patterns or even established theories. The average age of Nobel Prize laureates has been increasing over a long period, reaching 68 years today.

John Goodenough, an American physicist and chemist specializing in magnetism and superconductivity, received Nobel Prize in Physics in 2019, at the age of 97, for his work on lithium-ion batteries, thus becoming the oldest laureate. Some particularly brilliant and precocious researchers quickly gain fame, like mathematician **Jean-Pierre Serre**, who ranked first in the Mathematics Agrégation at the age of 22 and received the Fields Medal at 27. At 29, he was elected to the Collège de France. But for many others, the path to fame through scientific or medical research proves to be much longer.

For instance, **Pierre Agostini**, a French physicist born in 1941, recently received the Nobel Prize in Physics in 2023 at the age of 82 for his work on attosecond technology, alongside two other laureates, including the Franco-Swedish **Anne L'Huillier**. On this occasion, he expressed regret for having had to retire twenty years earlier and to exile himself to the United States when he still had plenty of energy.

Another case of late recognition in international fame is that of biologist **Luc Montagnier,** awarded the Nobel Prize in Medicine at the age of 76 for his discovery of the HIV virus, along with **Françoise Barré-Sinoussi** and **Harald zur Hausen.** Later, Luc Montagnier would be more under the media spotlight for some controversies regarding the origin of the Covid-19 pandemic, which he attributed to human creation in a laboratory, for his statements in favor of the anti-VAX lobby, and for his support of homeopaths and the theory of water memory. Note that at the age of 65, Luc Montagnier is obliged, by French law, to retire and leave the Pasteur Institute. The affair caused a scandal, and as he totally rejected the idea of retirement, he went into exile in the United States, and then later in China at Shanghai University to continue his work. Professor Montagnier passed away at the American Hospital in Neuilly-sur-Seine in 2022 at the age of 89, leaving behind a mixed legacy of a brilliant researcher who veered into conspiracy theories and unproven medical theories in his later life.

Another case of late fame is **Louis Pasteur**. He was born in December 1822 in Dole, Jura. After completing his two baccalaureates in literature and mathematical sciences, he defended his doctoral thesis in sciences at the Faculty of Sciences in Paris. Then he became an assistant professor at the Faculty of Sciences in Strasbourg. He married the rector's daughter and had five children with her. In 1853, at the age of 31, the Republic distinguished him for the first time by awarding him the Legion of Honor, and a year later, he went to Lille as the dean of the Faculty of Sciences, where he worked on the fermentation of beer, lactic fermentation, and diseases of wine. All of these works would pave the way for techniques of pasteurization and food preservation. Pasteur, long a close associate of Emperor Napoleon III, became a Commander of the Legion of Honor in 1868 after suffering a stroke that left him with lifelong effects. He was promoted to Grand Officer ten years later. In 1882, Louis Pasteur was elected to the French Academy, just as his team had developed a vaccine against anthrax in sheep. But it was truly from 1885, at the age of 63, that he achieved genuine international fame with the discovery of the rabies vaccine. He died at the age of 73 near Garches in France, and national funerals were organized to pay him a final tribute.

Vernon Lomax Smith is a 97-year-old American economist who still teaches economics and finance at Chapman University in California. Smith continues to publish research, write books, and constantly travel across the United States to give lectures to various audiences. He is or has been a board member of various major economic journal publishers, including the American Economic Review. Passionate about economics, Vernon Smith taught the subject for years at various American universities, including Arizona State University and George Mason University in Virginia. In 2002, Vernon was awarded the Nobel Prize in Economic Sciences at the age of 76. Recently, Vernon Smith stated, *"I think I've never been as good or better than I am now. Partly because I* *have more knowledge in various areas than my younger colleagues who are still in a learning process."*

Peter W. Higgs was born on May 29, 1929, in Newcastle, United Kingdom. His mother is Scottish, and his father has a job as a sound engineer at the BBC. Young Peter had fragile health, suffering from asthma, and as a child, he had to receive his education at home because of this condition. From the age of 17, he studied mathematics and physics until obtaining a PhD at King's College London in 1954. After a few years during which he will work in London, he returns to settle at the University of Edinburgh, for good this time In 1964, Peter Higgs, along with two other researchers, **François Englert** and **Robert Brout,** proposed a theory to explain why most particles have mass. Higgs and his colleagues theorized that an, as yet unidentified, boson plays a key role in this quantum physics phenomenon. This theory was outlined in two of Higgs' publications in 1964, titled "Broken Symmetries, Mass-less Particles and Gauge Fields" and "Broken Symmetries and the Masses of Gauge Bosons." At that time, Higgs was a lecturer in mathematical and physical sciences at the University of Edinburgh. Peter Higgs began to receive various awards after the age of fifty, notably the Hughes Medal from the Royal Society in 1981, and the Rutherford Medal from the Institute of Physics in 1984. However, it was especially after the age of sixty that he received the most recognition, culminating in the Nobel Prize in Physics in 2013, shared with François Englert, when he was already 84 years old. Even before receiving the Nobel Prize, Higgs gained international renown in 2008 when, following a series of experiments at the Large Hadron Collider at CERN in Geneva, Switzerland, the existence of the Higgs boson described by the theory was proven. The confirmation of this proof came in 2013. Peter Higgs passed away in April 2024, at the age of 94.

WAY NUMBER FIVE

WAY NUMBER FIVE : GOING INTO SPACE

Space tourism undoubtedly has a bright future, given the rapid advancements in space technology and the widespread interest in the exploration and discovery of the cosmos. In addition to the International Space Station (ISS), which hosted its first space tourist **Dennis Tito** in April 2001 when he was 60, other players are already positioning themselves in this future lucrative market, such as SpaceX, Blue Origin, and Virgin Galactic. More modestly, stratospheric flights conducted by rockets or spacecraft like New Shepard or VSS Unity have welcomed celebrities such as **Jeff Bezos** or **Richard Branson**. The Russians are not left behind, as some Soyuz missions have already allowed an actress and a filmmaker to join the International Space Station.

The story of **Jon Goodwin** deserves to be recalled. Born in 1943 in England, he participated in the Munich Olympics in 1972 as a canoeist and held various records in this specialty during expeditions in the USA, the Himalayas, and the Arctic. Jon Goodwin was diagnosed with Parkinson's disease in 2014. While battling this disease, he helped others through donations. In 2023, at the age of 80, he boarded the Virgin Galactic spacecraft and took off from New Mexico with two other space tourists, a mother and her daughter. He thus became the first Olympic participant to travel into space. Goodwin had purchased his space ticket in 2005 for $250,000, long before his illness was diagnosed, and his flight could only take place nine years after it was diagnosed. During this interval, he thought that his dream would never come true, especially because he feared that Virgin Galactic would cancel his flight due to his physical condition, which Virgin Galactic did not do. Although the Virgin Galactic spacecraft VSS Unity, which is launched from a carrier aircraft called White Knight Two, only performs suborbital flights up to 80 km in altitude, it allows its passengers to experience weightlessness for a few minutes.

Similarly, the American **Wally Funk** became famous in July 2021, at the age of 82, by also completing a suborbital flight during the Blue Origin New Shepard-16 mission, reaching an altitude of 107 km. Wally Funk made her flight in good company as the crew of the spacecraft included Jeff Bezos, his brother Mark, and an 18-year-old, Oliver Daemen, who thus became the youngest person to fly into space. It must be said that Wally Funk was no stranger to aviation, as she had obtained her pilot's license at the age of 17. Although highly skilled in piloting various aircraft ranging from gliders to seaplanes, she could not become a commercial pilot or a fighter pilot in the US Air Force just because, at that time, women were not allowed to pursue such careers. She became, however, an instructor and later an inspector at the Federal Aviation Administration (FAA). The fact that the Russians began sending women into space with Valentina Tereshkova in 1963, then Svetlana Savitskaya in 1982 and 1984 (the first woman to perform a spacewalk), finally convinced the American NASA to do the same in 1984. Moreover, NASA, since its establishment in 1958, had never explicitly excluded women from its training programs. Starting from 2007, the US Congress recognized the contribution of Wally Funk and her colleagues.

WAY NUMBER SIX

WAY NUMBER SIX: INFLUENCING ON **SOCIAL MEDIA**

Increasingly, seniors are also joining social networks to publish content, which is often aimed at people much younger than themselves. They are called "grandfluencers." Born in 1928 during the Great Depression, **Helen Van Winkle** lost her husband Earl in a car accident on their 35th wedding anniversary. In 1999, Helen's son, David, died at the age of 46 after a brief battle with cancer, a loss that Helen still finds difficult to comprehend. *"I fought for years trying to overcome the death of my son and husband,"* admits Helen. *"I led a very sad life, but I had to look like I was okay and be strong for my daughter, my five grandchildren, and my three great grandchildren."* She became an internet sensation at the age of eighty-five by uploading an image on Twitter, wearing her great-granddaughter's clothes. Following this, she was followed by singer **Rihanna** on social media, and success followed. Her catchphrase on the Web *"Stealing yo man since 1928"* became momentarily famous in 2016. Her Instagram account, baddie-winkle, currently has 3.2 million followers. She is known for her humor and for fighting ageism through her own style, wearing whimsical clothing. Winkle is a lobbyist whose self-expression is a statement of dissatisfaction with the sector of excellence and the false restrictions it imposes on people, especially women. She has a large following through online entertainment, where she posts photographs and recordings of herself, often with intriguing dresses with exceptional prints, or small outfits to support body positivism.

Less followed than Helen Van Winkle, **Studio Danielle**, in France, (1.1 million followers on Instagram) consists of a duo composed of Danielle, 69 years old, and Arthur, 38 years her junior. Danielle's straightforward talk and a certain form of naivety initially won over Arthur when Danielle was the caregiver for his grandfather. The duo met in 2013, and Studio Danielle started in October 2015, making Danielle one of the most famous grandmas on the Internet. On Facebook, Danielle gets involved in various topics ranging from chocolate soufflé to VAT payment, as well as silly bets with her partner Arthur or scenes at the sea or in the mountains. Arthur and Danielle made their debut in July 2022 as contestants on the TV show Fort Boyard.

Shirley Curry, who goes by the nickname "Skyrim Grandma," is an American You Tuber who became known in the world of video games. Shirley Curry was born in 1936 and retired in 1991 after working successively in a candy factory and in the clothing department of the Kmart Corporation. At the age of 60, Shirley delved into the world of video games thanks to her son, who introduced her to the strategy game Civilization II, which had just been released. She then followed video game groups on YouTube and made videos about Skyrim, a game that allows players to freely explore a virtual world and embark on personal adventures. Quickly, Shirley amassed subscribers to her video channel, surpassing one million in 2022, the year she unfortunately suffered a stroke during her sleep. Since then, she has been recovering from this health accident. Although she forgot how to play, she has expressed her wishes for the future of her residence in Ohio.

WAY NUMBER SEVEN

WAY NUMBER SEVEN: RADIO-TELEVISION OR ADVER-TISING

On January 17, 1989, buried in the Cemetery of Saint-Hymer near Pont-l'Évêque in Calvados (France), an old washerwoman named **Jeanne-Marie Le Calvé** is laid to rest. Jeanne-Marie is then 95 years old and has worked all her life, first as a level crossing keeper, then as a washerwoman at the end of World War II. Initially married to an employee of the Compagnie des Chemins de Fer de l'Ouest, Yves Marie Denis, whom she divorced in 1939 after having five children with him, she started a new life with another man who will die in the bombings. It was in 1972, under the pseudonym **"La Mère Denis,"** that Jeanne Marie, then 79 years old, entered television fame by becoming the face of a TV advertising campaign promoting the Vedette washing machine brand. Between 1972 and 1980, La Mère Denis became known to 80% of the French population. Advertising executive Jacques Séguéla was enthusiastic upon discovering La Mère Denis's advertisements, which focused on a return to the land, authenticity, and the timeless France with its flagship slogan : *"Ça, c'est vrai ça!"* pronounced *"Ch'est ben vrai cha!"* (« *That's very true indeed ! »*) Séguéla said of this advertising campaign: *"It's the campaign I would have loved to create."* La Mère Denis's natural charm quickly elevated her to the status of an advertising star, even as she promoted the Vedette brand. In 1976, at the age of 83, she was a guest on Bernard Pivot's show Apostrophes, and then designated the most remarkable personality of the year by Paris Match magazine.,She was caricatured by the cartoonist Cabu, appeared in a sketch by the comedian Coluche, became the muse of a cookbook, and even had a portrait in The New York Times in 1976. Having become somewhat the grandmother of the French, she passed away in 1989 at the age of 95, after living her old age comfortably thanks to the income from her advertising appearances.

In July 1913, **Germaine Soleil** was born in the twelfth arrondissement of Paris and became the eldest of four children. Born into a poor family, she began working at the age of 12 to help her family make ends meet and took on various odd jobs. At 20, she became the secretary of a notorious swindler, Serge Alexandre Stavisky, a Frenchman of Russian origin, and responsible for one of the biggest financial scandals of the 20th century. He was found dying in a chalet in Chamonix, his death never truly elucidated, whether suicide or murder. From that period, even before the Stavisky scandal erupted, forcing him to flee, Germaine Soleil was convinced of having extrasensory abilities. Germaine married, but when her husband returned from the war, their little family was ruined, and poverty resettled. A showman then became convinced of Germaine's psychic talents. Germaine, with his help, was able to exercise this ability in a caravan. After a few years like this, success finally came, and she attracted a loyal clientele on Boulevard Poissonnière in Paris, where she set up her fortune-telling practice. In 1970, at the age of 57, thanks to one of her regular clients, she managed to meet the manager of Europe 1, who offered her the opportunity to intervene daily on the microphone of this famous and popular radio station. The show was an immediate audience hit, with Madame Soleil providing astrological predictions for each zodiac sign. Germaine Soleil thus settled behind the microphone of the radio station Europe 1 for 23 years, such was the lasting success. Her clientele extended to a population of personalities from the political, business, and showbiz worlds. In 1971, the French **President Georges Pompidou** added, if it was needed, to Germaine's notoriety by responding to a question about France's future during a press conference, *"I don't know, I'm not Madame Soleil."* Madame Soleil also knew how to capture the attention of young children by becoming the official astrologer of the TV show Club Dorothée. In the late 1980s, she participated in Jacques Martin's Sunday show, Le monde est à vous. Germaine Soleil passed away on October 27, 1996, in Levallois- Perret at the age of 83.

More generally, it is clear that working in television or radio keeps those who do it going, as seen with the radio/TV host **Larry King,** who recently passed away at the age of 87 but was still regularly appearing on airwaves a few months before his death. Also in France, **Michel Drucker**, 81 years old, remains faithful to his position despite serious health issues, and **Alain Duhamel**, 84 years old, who has just given up a regular columnist role on BFM TV. We could also mention **Oprah Gail Winfrey**, 70 years old, more than ever an icon as one of the most influential woman in the world, or **Anna Wintour,** 74 ans, media executive and the editor- in-chief of Vogue. This proves that when talent and passion for one's profession are combined, there is no age limit, and success achieved at a younger age persists.

WAY NUMBER EIGHT

WAY NUMBER EIGHT : BECOMING AN ACADEMICIAN OR RECEIVING A LITERARY AWARD

It seems that until 1981, the toilets at the Institut de France, on Quai de Conti in Paris, were exclusively for men. Why indeed provide mixed toilets when this noble institution only welcomed men ? But in 1980, **Marguerite Yourcenar**, then 76 years old, was elected to the Académie Française, becoming the first woman to sit there, succeeding Roger Caillois. Supported in her election by the French writer and novelist Jean d'Ormesson and against the majority of her colleagues attached to the academy's masculine tradition, the latter, when asked by an American journalist what this election would change, declared: *"From now on there will be two toilets, one for the gentlemen, one for Madame Yource-nar."* This election cemented Marguerite Yourcenar's national and international fame, although the publication of her novel Memoirs of Hadrian in 1951 was a worldwide success and established her reputation as a major writer. This novel earned her various literary awards including the Femina-Vacaresco Prize, the French Academy Prize, and an American prize. While she had already received the Femina Prize in 1968 for The Abyss (L'OEuvre au noir), in 1977 she was distinguished with the Grand Prize of the French Academy for her entire body of work. In 1986, she was made Commander of the Legion of Honor. Marguerite Yourcenar died in December 1987 in Bangor, USA, at the age of 84.

Annie Ernaux was born in Normandy in 1940. She published her first novel, Cleaned Out (Les Armoires Vides) in 1974, which deals with abortion and is partly autobiographical. She later revisited this subject in The Event (L'Événement). Ten years later, in 1984, she won the Renaudot Prize for her novel A Man's Place, also autobiographical about her parental relationships. In 2008, she published The Years, a book where she speaks of herself in the third person, which notably earned her the Prix de la langue française. To be direct, although Annie Ernaux enjoyed recognition in literary circles due to her works, she remained largely unknown to the general public until October 6, 2022, when, at the age of 82, she was awarded the Nobel Prize in Literature by the King of Sweden, Carl XVI Gustav. From then on, in addition to immediate international recognition, her book sales multiplied tenfold across all her works available in bookstores. Annie Ernaux is not the first woman to benefit later in life from international celebrity thanks to receiving a Nobel Prize. We can also mention the cases of the Polish poet **Wisława Szymborska**, crowned with the prestigious prize in 1996 at the age of 73, or that of **Alice Munro,** the first Canadian woman to be distinguished with the Nobel at the age of 82 for her short stories describing the ordinary life of "normal people."

Katherine Anne Porter was born in May 1890 in Indian Creek, a very little unincorporated Community in west-central

Texas.

She lost her mother at the age or two and subsequently, she had to endure her father's neglect.

The first of her four successive husbands was John Henry Koontz, whom she married at the age of fifteen years. Koonz was violent and abusive, so Katherine divorced in 1915, the same year she was falsely diagnosed with tuberculosis. She had to spend two years in sanatorium while she only suffered from bronchitis. At this time, she decided to become a writer

During her early twenties, she moved from Texas to Chicago where she worked briefly as an extra in movies. She supported herself as a journalist and ghost writer.

Traveling back and forth between Mexico and New York City, Katherine Anne Porter published her first short-story collection Flowering Judas and Other Stories in 1930, at the age of 40.

During her intimate personal life, she suffered several miscarriages, had an abortion, contracted gonorrhea from an English painter, and had a hysterectomy, all things putting an end to her hopes of ever having a child.

From the 1930s to the 1950s, she continued to publish short stories and became a prominent figure on the American literary scene, despite the fact that her sales were insufficient to allow her to survive without advances and grants.

In 1939, she published her second book, a collection of three short novels, Pale Horse, Pale Rider, followed in 1944 with another book titled The Leaning Tower and Other Stories.

Between 1948 and 1958, she taught at Stanford University and other famous universities after having been for a long time writer-in residence at several colleges and universities such as University of Chicago, University of Michigan and University of Virginia.

Interested in the reasons which allowed the rise of Nazism, her first and only novel Ship of Fools, published in 1962, was an immediate success. Katherine Anne was 72 years old at this time. This best-seller became a major film in 1965.

The same year in 1965, Porter's Collected Short Stories won the National Book Award and the Pulitzer Prize for fiction.

In 1977 she published The Never-Ending Wrong, about the trial and execution of Sacco and Vanzetti, which she had denounced decades before.

Shortly after she had a serious stroke and three years later, she died in Maryland at the age of 90.

WAY NUMBER NINE

WAY NUMBER NINE : BECOMING THE "HERO" OF A CRISIS OR ENTREPRENEURIAL SAGA

In September 1890, in a farm in Indiana, **Harland David Sanders** was born, the first of three children. His father died when he was only five years old, leaving his mother, a simple housekeeper, to care for him and his siblings. She had to work at night to improve the family's meager income. Harland David took advantage of this time to cook and learn basic culinary recipes. He was passionate about it. His mother remarried a food producer, and Harland became a farm laborer until adolescence. After a brief stint as a streetcar conductor, he joined the US Army and served in Cuba. He then worked various odd jobs before starting a steamboat company on the Ohio River. He later opened a carbide lamp manufacturing business but quickly went bankrupt due to the expansion of rural electrification. Penniless, he found a job as a railroad worker in Illinois and obtained a law degree from a university, which allowed him to become a justice of the peace after being laid off from the railroad in 1915. Things went well for him until he was removed from his position as a judge after fighting with a client in the courtroom. In 1930, at the age of 40, he moved with his family to Kentucky and took over the management of a Shell gas station. He cooked for his customers and served them at home because there was no restaurant at the gas station. The dishes served were simple— chicken, fries, ham, mashed potatoes, and biscuits—but they were delicious and popular. So much so that in 1931, he opened Sanders Cafe, a 142-seat restaurant where he acted as a one-man band: head chef, cashier, and gas station attendant. He even found time to take management courses at Cornell University and was bestowed the title of "Kentucky Colonel" by the governor of Kentucky because he honored local cuisine. Customers eventually came more for the homemade chicken than to fill their gas tanks. Since he also operated a motel, he set up a bedroom and a showcase toilet in the restaurant to encourage customers to stay overnight. In 1939, the "Colonel," who was approaching his fifties, hit the jackpot when a famous food critic celebrated his establishment, Sanders Court and Café, in his gastronomic guide. Following this success, Sanders improved his fried chicken recipe by adding herbs and spices and using a pressure cooker to shorten cooking times. His "Colonel" title serves to build a character who becomes "Colonel Sanders," and he dresses in Southern colors. World War II forced him to close the motel in 1942, but he retained the idea that the formula still had potential in the form of franchises. Chicken restaurants began to expand under the impetus of Peter Harman, an entrepreneur with whom Sanders had worked on the franchising project. A brand was created, and it became Kentucky Fried Chicken, accompanied by the slogan *"finger-lickin' good."* The bucket of fries became the typical side dish, and it was successful until a highway project caused the value of his businesses to collapse, leaving him bankrupt again at the age of 66. He survived for a while on modest Social Security payments, then resumed his travels across America in his old Ford to convince new franchisees. Legend has it that he tried over a thousand times to persuade a restaurant to invest in his recipe. Nonetheless, by sheer determination, in 1963, the Kentucky Fried Chicken chain began to generate significant profits. In 1959, he sold his business to investors close to the governor of Kentucky and became the brand's official ambassador. He appeared in all advertisements and traveled worldwide, engaging in charitable works and adopting nearly 80 orphaned foreign children. In 1969, at the age of 79, he could take pride in seeing Kentucky Fried Chicken go public. He fell out with the brand when he wanted to use his name to open his restaurant and eventually had to do so under his wife's name. Although he had to close it in the 1980s, a survey named him one of the most popular people in the world, and he published a book titled *"My Life, As I Have Lived It, Has Been Finger- Lickin' Good."* He died of leukemia at the age of 90, and all restaurants worldwide then flew their flags at half-mast. The recipe for his chicken and its eleven herbs and spices, unchanged since 1940, remains a closely guarded secret and is kept in a unique copy in a safe at the company's headquarters.

At the age of 63, in 2005, **Didier Lombard** became CEO of France Telecom, later renamed Orange. He succeeded Thierry Breton, who was then appointed Minister of Economy, Finance, and Industry in the French government. Until then, Didier Lombard was known only within the very closed circle of the telecommunications and computer industry and the boards of directors of major CAC 40 stock index companies. Graduate of the École Polytechnique and the École Nationale Supérieure des Télécommunications, he began his career at the Centre National des Télécommunications (CNET), a big R&D division, in 1967, eventually becoming the director of one of its centers before transitioning to the Ministry of Industry after stints at industrial groups such as Bull and Thomson. His appointment at the helm of France Telecom certainly brought him national prominence in France and international recognition in the telecom industry. However, it was actually on an entirely different matter, one that Didier Lombard would have undoubtedly preferred to avoid, that his name would make headlines in the media and social networks for weeks: the France Telecom suicides affair. As some media outlets revealed that several dozen people were committing suicide each year, notably at their workplace at France Telecom due to a relentless and authoritarian internal restructuring plan known as NEXT. Didier Lombard made a major communication blunder in September 2009 during a press conference following his meeting with Labor Minister Xavier Darcos. He indeed stated his intention *"to stop to this trend of suicides that shocks everyone."* Faced with an avalanche of outraged reactions to the suggestion that suicide could be a trend, Didier Lombard was forced to backtrack the next day, committing yet another communication blunder during his apology on RTL. He then claimed to have mistakenly used the word "trend," which was a French analogy of the English word "mood." Of course, this convoluted excuse convinced no one and only fueled the media frenzy further. Old statements by Didier Lombard resurfaced. While the NEXT plan aimed to eliminate 22,000 positions between 2006 and 2008, he had declared to a gathering of executives: *"I will get rid of these departures through the door or through the window."* This resurfacing statement took on an even more macabre turn when, in September 2009, a 32-year-old employee of the group, Stéphanie, jumped from a window at her workplace in Paris. Initially forced to relinquish the position of CEO to Stéphane Richard, who would eventually replace him entirely, Didier Lombard eventually announced his resignation as Chairman of the Board of Directors of Orange, and later as Special Advisor in March 2011. After an initial conviction for institutional moral harassment, Didier Lombard saw his sentence reduced in September 2022 by the Paris Court of Appeal.

In 1930, in Omaha, Nebraska, **Warren Buffet** was born to a homemaker mother and a stockbroker father, a member of the U.S. Congress. Early on, fascinated by financial markets and influenced by his father's brokerage work, Warren bought his first stock at the age of 11 and declared his first income at 13. After university studies, first in Pennsylvania, then in Nebraska, and finally at Columbia University in New York, where he met investor Benjamin Graham, he became interested in undervalued companies in the stock market but with real value (value investing). Determining the true value of a company by thoroughly investigating its financial ratios would be Warren Buffet's hallmark throughout his investing career and the essential reason for his success. At the age of 26, Warren Buffet founded his own company, Buffet Associates. He became a millionaire at 30. He bought a struggling textile mill, Berkshire Hathaway, cheaply in 1962, using this investment as a vehicle for further investments always based on the principle of acquiring undervalued companies by the market. The shares of Berkshire Hathaway, which were then worth $8, eventually reached $550,000. Buffet then ventured into life insurance, using the fact that life insurance companies always have cash-flow in advance because premiums are always paid by policyholders before the invested funds become payable. Subsequently, Warren did not stop and invested in prestigious firms such as Coca-Cola, American Express, Apple, or Bank of America. Known for his frugality and modest lifestyle despite his fortune, now estimated at $120 billion, 93-year-old Warren Buffet has promised to donate his entire fortune to charitable organizations in coordination with his friend Bill Gates. Nicknamed "the Oracle of Omaha," Warren has become one of the richest men in the world, without inheriting wealth and after once being a street vendor for Coca-Cola. Later he sold cigarettes and magazines in addition to Coca Cola cans and invested all his savings in stocks. After becoming a millionaire at 30, Warren took advantage of the oil crisis of the 1970s to acquire businesses at discounted prices. Thus, Warren became a billionaire at 56 and over time became a major source of inspiration for investors, knowing that his time management is a major element of his success. He often says that *"the stock market is a means of transferring money from the impatient to the patient."* His ability to wait for the right opportunities and to hold onto his positions for the long term is legendary. In 1999, at the age of 69, Warren was recognized as the best investor of the 20th century. At 78, his fortune surpassed that of his friend Bill Gates, founder of Microsoft, and he became the 5th richest man in the world in 2022. Now 93 years old, Warren Buffet remains a monument of international finance and an oracle always highly listened to by investors and financial specialists.

Didier Raoult was born in 1952 in Dakar, Senegal, to a father who was a doctor from Brittany and a mother who was a nurse from Marseille, herself the granddaughter of a renowned Parisian hospital doctor and infectious disease specialist. This medical heritage directed him, after rather mediocre secondary studies, towards a medical career, after completing his internship at the Faculty of Medicine in Marseille. Unable to become an obstetrician as he would have liked given his ranking in the competition, he became an infectious disease specialist like his maternal great-grandfather, Paul Le Gendre. Specializing in the study of viruses and bacteria, he was awarded the Grand Prize of the INSERM (National Institute of Health and Medical Research) in 2010, an award that France tributes to a researcher whose work has led to significant progress in the fields of human physiology, therapy, and more broadly in the field of health. While Didier Raoult enjoys recognition among medical research circles and in the Marseille area, he has successively been a hospital practitioner at Aix-Marseille University, then director of the Hospital-University Institute Mediterranean Infection from 2011 to 2022. He remains largely unknown to the general public, although he is well known among specialists in infectious diseases and microbiologists through his more than 2000 publications. He is thus one of the most prolific French researchers. It was in 2020, during the COVID-19 pandemic, that his national and international notoriety literally exploded. Indeed, Didier Raoult claims that COVID-19 can be effectively treated with a cheap drug long known to prevent malaria, hydroxychloroquine (HCQ). Didier Raoult gained significant support for his argument from the American President Donald Trump, who in turn promotes this drug as a "COVID-killer." Pretty soon, Didier Raoult emerged as an international figure in alternative medicine to mRNA vaccines. Things start to sour for Didier Raoult when several facts begin to emerge, questioning his professional ethics: · Didier Raoult allegedly conducted blood sampling on homeless and vulnerable populations for bacteriological analysis and publication in scientific journals as early as 1993, without obtaining any necessary authorizations to involve human beings in such a process. The argument put forward by Professor Didier Raoult to justify this was that it was not about conducting a research protocol, but merely providing care. · This same argument will be used for clinical trials conducted on more than 30,000 patients during the COVID epidemic. Didier Raoult and his team claim that based on early diagnosis, isolation, and early treatment of at least three days with hydroxychloroquine, this leads to better avoidance of severe forms and a faster reduction in viral load than with any other treatment. However, two damning reports will be detailed, one by the National Agency for the Safety of Medicines (ANSM), and the other by the General Inspectorate of Social Affairs (IGAS), which will debunk these claims and highlight illegal practices and scientific studies at the IHU

Méditerranée, of which Didier Raoult is the Director. · Moreover, Professor Raoult is the subject of defamation lawsuits or harassment towards a researcher and his own daughter. The latter, Magali Carcopino-Tusoli, with whom he had a permanent falling out during a family quarrel, said of him in an interview with the newspaper L'Express: *"My father dreamed of the Nobel Prize, he became the leader of conspiracy theorists."*

WAY NUMBER TEN

WAY NUMBER TEN: SLIPPING INTO DELINQUENCY

In 1965, the man who was the oldest death row inmate in France passed away from lung congestion at the hospice hospital in Digne-les-Bains in the Alpes de Haute Provence, at the age of 88. His name? **Gaston Dominici**. It all began on August 5, 1952, when the bodies of an English couple and their ten-year-old daughter, the Drummonds, were found near the village of Lurs in the Alpes de Haute Provence. They had been shot several times with a rifle around one in the morning, while they had stopped the previous evening by the roadside to spend the night in their car on their vacation journey. The skull of the little girl was smashed with the butt of a rifle. Very quickly, the suspicions of the investigators turned to Gaston Dominici, a 75-year-old peasant whose farm was located 150 meters from the crime scene. Gaston Dominici confessed to the triple murder, then retracted his statement, claiming that he wanted to sacrifice himself to protect his two sons, Clovis and Gustave Dominici. The case quickly stirred considerable emotion, both due to the atrocious nature of the crime, the personality of the accused, the successive lies of the protagonists, the international aspect, as the victims were English, and the lack of motive, evidence, or murder weapon against Gaston Dominici. Gaston Dominici, born in January 1877, was 75 years old at the time and would subsequently make headlines in both national and international judicial chronicles. Rumors are running wild: some claimed that one of the victims, Jack Drummond, was actually a secret agent, an expert in chemical weapons, and a member of British intelligence, and that he was assassinated by a military commando from the special services. It so happened that a chemical factory, which Jack Drummond might have been interested in, was located near the village of Lurs. Gaston's two sons, Gustave and Clovis, successively accused their father of the triple murder, then retracted their statements in turn. From then on, confusion and doubt settled in people's minds; guilty or innocent? All of this in an old-fashioned rural environment (Gaston was nicknamed the Patriarch of Grand Terre) and the extraordinary personality of the accused, a true clan leader, perfectly portrayed by the actor Jean Gabin in the film The Dominici Affair in 1973. The investigating commissioner, Edmond Sébeille, a young police officer from the 9th mobile brigade of Marseille, was himself a character and was nicknamed the "Marseille Maigret." For the Justice system, there was hardly any doubt: Gaston Dominici was guilty. He was sentenced to death in 1954, even though he proclaimed his innocence throughout the trial. His sentence was later commuted to life imprisonment due to his advanced age, and then he was pardoned by the French President General de Gaulle and released on July 14, 1960, after spending six years in Baumettes Prison in Marseille. Even today, doubt persists about Gaston Dominici's actual guilt in this exceptional criminal case. Outre the 1973 film directed by Claude Bernard-Aubert, starring Jean Gabin, the Dominici affair fueled the headlines of numerous newspapers, radios, and TV shows for years, both in France and abroad, thus making Gaston Dominici famous in a way he could never have imagined.

Bernard Madoff, also known as Bernie Madoff, was born on April 29, 1938, in New York City, Queens, to a modest family of immigrant origins. His grandparents were indeed from Eastern Europe. After attending Far Rockaway High School, he enrolled at the University of Alabama in 1956 but only stayed for a year. He then transferred to Hofstra University and earned a Bachelor of Arts in political science. He later attended law school for a year at Brooklyn Law School before permanently leaving the educational system to found his own company, Bernard L. Madoff Investment Securities LLC. He operated as a stockbroker and started with only $5,000. Since his firm was not a member of the New York Stock Exchange (NYSE), he bypassed its rules. Over time, with the help of his brother Peter, his company attracted more and more orders from other brokers by offering them compensation for their orders made possible by the difference between bid and ask prices (the "payment for order flow" mechanism). Madoff managed to make better deals than other market makers and even the NYSE, especially by being ahead of others in using digital technologies, allowing him to be faster and more competitive than his rivals. Based on his financial successes, Madoff participated in numerous regulatory and financial association meetings such as the Securities Industry Association (SIA). In 1971, a certain Gordon Macklin also wanted to use digital technologies. To trade certain securities, he would be instrumental in the creation of NASDAQ. Surprisingly, given what follows, the Securities and Exchange Commission (SEC), the U.S. regulator, viewed Madoff's opening up to more competition, especially for market makers at the NYSE, rather favorably. Madoff and his brother took advantage of this to strengthen their relations with SEC lawyers and officials, including by giving them tours of their small trading room and instilling confidence in their own activities. In 1987, under the Reagan Administration, a market crisis occurred, providing Bernie Madoff with the opportunity to become co-chairman of NASDAQ and to suggest improvement recommendations, given his recognized expertise. Bernie Madoff was then involved in all trading committees due to his knowledge of market structures, enhancing his credibility everywhere. The head of the NYSE and Bernie Madoff eventually got along famously. At the same time, Bernie Madoff sponsored events for the SIA and even provided them with office space after the September 11 attacks on the World Trade Center. As a result, Bernie and his brother Peter enjoyed such trust from regulatory bodies that they were very little inclined to scrutinize the activities of Bernard L. Madoff Investment Securities. Madoff attracted wealthy investors by promising them significant and continuous returns through an investment strategy called split-strike conversion, a strategy that was legal. Deeply connected in the New York Jewish community, Madoff attracted rich and prestigious investors such as certain charitable funds (Elie Wiesel Foundation for Peace, the global women's charity Hadassah) or personalities from showbiz, cinema, or media (John Malkovich, Kevin Bacon, Jeffrey Katzenberg from Dreamworks, Larry King, or Steven Spielberg). Just in 2008, right before the scandal, Madoff's company announced annual returns up by 5.6%, while at the same time the Standard and Poor's (S&P) index dropped by 39%. In 2008, the scandal erupted, although prior warnings had been issued as early as 2000 and 2005 by a financial analyst, Harry Markopolos, to the SEC, warnings that were ignored by the SEC. The reality is that Madoff constructed a fraudulent financial scheme called a Ponzi scheme, in which the investments acquired from clients are solely paid out with funds brought in by new clients. The system collapses when the financial contributions from new entrants prove insufficient to cover the payouts to existing clients. Bernard Madoff and his company, therefore, did not actually make any financial investments on behalf of the clients he enticed with promises of returns far above the market, but simply paid them by continuously attracting new clients to fuel the Ponzi scheme. The reversal of the financial markets from 2007 onwards in the United States, the infamous subprime crisis, proved fatal to Bernie Madoff and led to the collapse of his pyramid. The fraud had begun years earlier, perhaps as early as 1975, although Madoff claimed in court that he had initiated it only in 1990. Madoff deceived thousands of investors of tens of billions of dollars, thus becoming one of the greatest financial fraudsters of modern times. In 2011, the amount owed to clients amounted to $57 billion, knowing that at the beginning of the investigations, the fraud was estimated at $65 billion. More "reasonably,"a former SEC chairman, Harvey Pitt, later estimated that the net fraud was only in the range of $10 to $17 billion. Even though the subprime crisis was not caused by Bernie Madoff's actions, he nevertheless became its symbol and also a symbol of a finance gone mad, ravaged by the lure of easy and quick gains. This affair certainly made Madoff famous worldwide at the age of 70, and his trial was followed by journalists from around the world, especially since Madoff had funded Democratic Party politicians during his heyday and was heavily involved with the officials of the financial market regulatory authorities who were supposed to oversee him. He died in prison at the age of 82 from chronic illnesses in April 2021 at the Butner Correctional Complex in North Carolina.

In March 1952, a diamond cutter and his wife gave birth to Harvey in Queens, New York. Their name ? Max and Miriam Weinstein. Harvey soon welcomed a younger brother, Bob, into this Jewish family whose maternal grandparents were immigrants from Poland. **Harvey Weinstein**, after completing his secondary education at John Bowne High School, pursued higher education in Buffalo, New York, near Lake Erie. In the 1970s, Harvey and his brother Bob partnered in Buffalo to form a rock concert production company, Harvey and Corky Productions. Then, towards the end of the 1970s, using the profits they had made, they founded an independent film production company, Miramax, named after their parents. In the early 1980s, Miramax achieved its first success with the film The Secret Policeman's Other Ball, aimed at supporting the work of Amnesty International. It was especially in 1989, with the production of Sex, Lies, and Videotape,, a film directed by Steven Soderbergh and distributed by Miramax Films, which won the Palme d'Or at the Cannes Film Festival, that Miramax became one of the trendiest studios in the United States. In the 1990s, Miramax continued to grow by expanding its rights catalog and bringing Disney on board as a shareholder. In 1994, Miramax Films distributed Pulp Fiction , a thriller written and directed by Quentin Tarantino, featuring a prestigious cast including John Travolta, Samuel Jackson, Uma Thurman, Bruce Willis, and Rosanna Arquette. The film, entirely financed by Miramax, was a huge success, winning the Palme d'Or at Cannes and several Oscars at the 67th Academy Awards ceremony in Los Angeles. In 1997, commercial successes continued with films like Clerks, The English Patient, and Shakespeare in Love. In 2005, the Weinstein brothers left Miramax and founded The Weinstein Company (TWC), with Quentin Tarantino among others. Of course, by this time, Harvey Weinstein was well-known in all of Hollywood and more broadly in all cinema circles in North America and Europe. However, he remained largely unknown to the general public. In October 2017, The New York Times published an article detailing years of sexual harassment or assault perpetrated by Harvey Weinstein, with testimonies from actresses such as Rose McGowan and Ashley Judd. A few days later, thirteen more women testified in The New Yorker magazine, three of whom claimed to have been raped. Most of the complainants describe a fairly similar scenario. Weinstein receives young women in hopes of a role or casting in an upcoming film in his hotel room, where he begins to undress and take a shower. Then he asks for a massage and attempts to have sexual relations. Several of them, including actress Asia Argento, claim to have been raped by Harvey Weinstein. Very famous actresses such as Gwyneth Paltrow or Angelina Jolie subsequently state that they were sexually harassed by Weinstein when they were young. Then it's Cara Delevingne's turn to denounce inappropriate behavior by the producer towards her. Then British actress Lysette Anthony declares that she was raped in London in her apartment. Actress Brit Marling relates her fear and paralysis when during a first meeting in Harvey's hotel room to discuss a role, he suggests they take a shower together. At the end of October 2017, Georgina Chapman, Harvey Weinstein's wife, announced that she was filing for divorce. The avalanche of testimonies does not stop. On French television, Weinstein's personal driver, Mickael Chemloul, declares that he drove many aspiring actresses who seemed completely distraught after meeting Harvey Weinstein. Quentin Tarantino also tells The New York Times that he had been aware for years of Weinstein's abusive behavior towards women and that he should have done something to stop it. Actresses of different nationalities and living in various countries, including Norwegian actress Natassia Malthe, American actress Daryl Hannah (Kill Bill), or Mexican actress Lupita Nyong'o, all tell more or less the same scenario of inappropriate conduct, sexual harassment, or attempted rape by Harvey Weinstein. George Clooney and Matt Damon then speak out, saying that something must now change in Hollywood and that it is time for women's voices to be believed. The scandal does not stop and becomes international, making headlines in Western media. The Academy Awards votes to exclude Harvey Weinstein, he is forced to resign from the board of TWC, and the English and American justices are seized. It is revealed that Weinstein used private agents to exert pressure on the complainants and try to bribe them to withdraw their complaints. In 2018, Weinstein was indicted by the American justice system for rape and criminal sexual acts, and the trial took place in 2020. Although defended by the same lawyerfended the former leader of the IMF Dominique Strauss-Kahn (DSK), Benjamin Brafman, he was found guilty and sentenced to 23 years in prison, a sentence he received while sitting in a wheelchair at the age of 67. He was sentenced once again to 16 years in prison in February 2023 for the rape of an actress committed in Los Angeles in 2013. The international fame gained by the scandal was due as much to the impressive list of complainants and their fame (actresses, top models, production assistants) as to the fact that the scandal itself allowed the #MeToo movement, created in 2007 by African-American activist Tarana Burke, to assert itself worldwide and in all spheres, fromWall Street to Hollywood, through Silicon Valley, universities, businesses, politics, media, artistic and literary circles, etc. The feminist movement found its absolute repellent in the person of Harvey Weinstein and liberated women's voices to an unprecedented level. In 2019, the film Bombshell was released starring Charlize Theron and Nicole Kidman, which exposes the sexual harassment actions of Roger Ailes, one of the creators of the American television channel Fox News.

WAY NUMBER ELEVEN

WAY NUMBER ELEVEN : BECOMING HEAD OF STATE

In December 1906, in southern Ukraine near the Dnieper River, in Kamenskoye, a mining town, **Leonid Ilyich Brezhnev** was born into a family of workers from Kursk. He was 11 years old when the Russian Revolution broke out. Little is known about Leonid Ilyich's early years except that he began working at the age of 15 in the steel mill where his father already worked. Leonid became a member of the Communist Party of the Soviet Union in 1931 after studying at the Metallurgical Institute of Dnipropetrovsk (formerly Kamenskoye). He graduated as a qualified engineer, became the director of a technical school, all while holding various local positions within the party. Leonid capitalized on the Stalinist period by becoming a regional leader of the Communist Party for Dnipropetrovsk. He served his compulsory military service in an armored unit and served as a political commissar. He continued his political commissar activity in the Red Army during World War II until he became a major general in

1943, then responsible for political commissars for the Ukrainian front. Too young to have precise memories of pre-revolutionary Russia and having participated in the Leninist adventure, he adhered to Stalinism without any qualms. During the Nazi invasion, he became responsible for the political department of the 18th Army highly engaged on the Ukrainian front. His boss in the political hierarchy was then Nikita Khrushchev, who was the political commissar for the entire front under the supreme authority of Joseph Stalin. In fact, during the war, Leonid had much more of a career as an apparatchik than that of a military commander. In 1952, he became a member of the Central Committee of the Communist Party. He was then 46 years old and was ideally placed at the death of Stalin in 1953 as a protégé and confidant of Khrushchev, who succeeded Stalin as General Secretary of the Communist Party. In 1955, he was responsible for the Communist Party in Kazakhstan, then became the second secretary of the Central Committee, and then President of the Supreme Soviet in 1960, even though real power still lay in the hands of Khrushchev as the General Secretary of the party. Faithful to the latter until 1963, he switched to dissidence after the Cuban Missile Crisis, which weakened Khrushchev. A member of a network of conspirators, led by Anastas Mikoyan, Brezhnev contributed to Khrushchev's overthrow in 1964 and became the party's first secretary along with a duo, Alexei Kosygin and Mikoyan, respectively Prime Minister and Head of State. Brezhnev truly gained international fame in 1966, at the age of 60, when he became General Secretary, a role previously held by Stalin and of which Brezhnev would adopt the police methods by appointing a hardliner, Yuri Andropov, to head the KGB. The invasion of Czechoslovakia in 1968, the clashes between China and the USSR along the Ussuri River in 1969, and the unwavering support he provided to the Vietnamese in their conflict with America made him one of the most powerful leaders on the international scene. Under his leadership, the USSR rivaled the United States in the arms race and space exploration. But it was especially during what would be called "detente," a period of easing tensions between the USSR and the United States in the early 1970s, culminating in the joint signing by Richard Nixon of the first Strategic Arms Limitation Treaty (SALT I), then the Paris Accords that ended the Vietnam War. In 1973, and finally with the Helsinki Accords in 1975, which defined borders in Europe, Brezhnev left his mark on his country's history. In 1977, he pushed Podgorny, President of the Supreme Soviet Presidium, out the door and seized all power. In 1979, Brezhnev personally made the mistake of deciding to invade Afghanistan, closing the era of detente. Suffering a stroke in 1982, he died the same year of a heart attack at the age of 75.

Deng Xiaoping: without him, China would never have become what it is today, one of the world's leading economic powers. It was indeed Deng Xiaoping who embarked China on an unprecedented economic development path, with annual growth rates of over 10% continuously for years. Born in 1904 in Sichuan to a middle-class family of landowners, Deng Xiaoping, like Brezhnev, progressed within the hierarchy of the Chinese Communist Party. At the age of 15, he went to study in France, joined the Marxist youth, joined the Chinese Communist Youth League, and continued his studies in Moscow. He returned to China in 1927, integrated into the Chinese Communist Party (CCP), and participated in the Long March, the military retreat of the Chinese Red Army in the face of the advance of the nationalists during the civil war between 1934 and 1936. After the civil war and the war against Japan between 1937 and 1945, Mao Zedong founded the People's Republic of China in 1949 and forced the nationalist leader Chiang Kai-Shek to flee to Taiwan. Deng Xiaoping chose to support Mao from the beginning and found himself propelled to the position of General Secretary of the Party in 1954, at the age of 50. In 1958, Mao launched the "Great Leap Forward", a mass mobilization aimed at promoting agriculture and industrial production, but which resulted in famine and millions of deaths, perhaps 40 million between 1959 and 1961. This huge failure led to Mao's sidelining and allowed a quartet composed of Deng Xiaoping, Liu Shaoqi, Chen Yun, and Zhou Enlai to pursue a more liberal economic policy that slowly restored the economy, under Mao's disapproving gaze. Deng Xiaoping was much more discreet and pragmatic than Mao, and illustrating his liberal vision of the economy, he notably declared: *It doesn't matter if the cat is black or white, as long as it catches mice."* In 1966, weakened, Mao launched the "Cultural Revolution" in an attempt to regain control, aiming to purge society of its counter-revolutionary elements, which led to more than one and a half million additional deaths. By the late 1960s, Mao's health deteriorated, and during this episode, Deng Xiaoping became a target. He was excluded from the government and the party and forced to return to a rural province to work in a tractor factory. He remained in this purgatory for eight years until Zhou Enlai, himself very ill, convinced Mao to restore Deng Xiaoping's grace in 1974. He was exactly 70 years old when Mao appointed him Vice Premier Minister. When Zhou Enlai died in 1976, Deng Xiaoping again became the target of the famous "Gang of Four", instigators of the Cultural Revolution, supported covertly by Mao himself. It was only after Mao's death in September 1976 and the subsequent fall of the Gang of Four that Deng Xiaoping resumed his ascent within the party. In 1981, he became the undisputed leader of the People's Republic of China and the Chinese Communist Party. He remained in this position until 1992, when he resigned and was replaced by Jiang Zemin. Deng Xiaoping was one of the most important Chinese leaders whose initiative in 1978 to create special economic zones transformed China from a rigid socialist economy to a much more pragmatic and growth-oriented economy. Unfortunately, a lasting stain remains on Deng Xiaoping's record: the repression of Tienanmen Square in 1989, when thousands of students camped there demanding greater freedom of thought and expression. Deng Xiaoping, 85 years old at the time, nicknamed "the little helmsman" in opposition to Mao Zedong nicknamed "the great helmsman," was responsible for a repression that resulted in at least 1,800 deaths and tens of thousands of injuries, ending the "Beijing Spring." This event seriously tarnished Deng Xiaoping's international fame, but he still left a lasting legacy as one of the architects of modern China. His particularly active period was between his 77th and 85th years. He died in 1997 at the age of 92 from a lung infection and Parkinson's disease and had relatively modest funerals compared to those of Mao Zedong.

Rolihlahla Mandela was born in Mvezo near Cape Town, South Africa, on July 18, 1918, within the Madiba clan. His father was an advisor to a local king, the king of the Thembu people, Jongintaba Dalindyebo. When his father died, he was only 12 years old and became a ward of the king. In primary school, his teacher nicknamed him Nelson, following a custom of giving Christian names to students. Young Nelson continued his secondary education, then began university studies at the University College of Fort Hare, but failed to obtain the degree due to being expelled for participating in a student protest. This incident enraged King Jongintaba and later forced Nelson to move away and join Johannesburg. He worked in a mine as a security guard and eventually completed his university studies by acquiring his Bachelor's degree. He also attempted to obtain a law degree at the University of Witwatersrand but left in 1952 without the coveted diploma. He would successfully complete this training much later in 1989 during his time in prison. At the age of 26, Nelson Mandela joined the African National Congress (ANC), where he helped found its youth section (Youth League). He married a cousin in

1944 and had four children, two sons, and two daughters. Nelson pushed for the ANC to evolve towards a more radical mass action program starting in 1949, and in 1952, a civil disobedience campaign was launched against six laws considered unjust by both the ANC and the South African Indian Congress. Nelson Mandela was then sentenced to 9 months of community service, and later in 1956, he was arrested with several others during a police raid for treason. A lengthy trial, famous as The Treason Trial, followed, in which he was acquitted in 1961. Following racial riots in March 1960, during which the police killed 69 unarmed people, a state of emergency was declared, Nelson was arrested again, and the ANC and the Pan African Congress were dissolved. A national strike was scheduled in 1961, but postponed due to the massive mobilization of security forces, and Nelson Mandela was designated to lead the armed struggle against the authorities. Starting from 1962, Mandela traveled to garner support and received military training in Morocco and Ethiopia. Upon his return to South Africa, he was arrested for leaving the country without permission and inciting the strike. He was sentenced to 5 years in prison and was sent to detention in Pretoria. In 1963, during a trial for sabotage, he faced the death penalty along with other black activists and delivered a speech in 1964 that became famous, declaring, *"I have fought against white domination, and I have fought against black domination. I cherish the ideal of a democratic and free society in which all persons live together in harmony and with equal opportunities. It is an ideal which I hope to live for and to achieve. But if needs be, it is an ideal for which I am prepared to die."* On June 11, 1964, Nelson Mandela and seven other defendants were sentenced to life imprisonment. He was 46 years old. In 1968 and 1969, his mother and his young son Thembi passed away, and he was not allowed to attend their funerals. In 1988, he was diagnosed with tuberculosis, hospitalized for a few months, and then returned to prison until February 1990, the date of his release coinciding with the renewal of the ANC and Pan African Congress authorizations. He had spent 27 years in prison and was then 72 years old. His long struggle in prison propelled him to international fame. He was elected President of the ANC in 1991 and was awarded the Nobel Peace Prize jointly with President FW de Klerk. In May 1994, for the first time in his life, he was allowed to vote and was democratically elected as the first President of South Africa. In 1998, at the age of 80 and already divorced twice, he married his third wife, Graça Machel. Nelson Mandela resigned in 1999, honoring his promise to serve only one presidential term, and then focused on various charitable organizations he had launched, including a fund for children. He passed away in Johannesburg in December 2013 at the age of 95, having become a global symbol in the fight against apartheid.

When **Golda Meir** was born in 1898 in Kiev, Ukraine, to a family that economic difficulties forced to immigrate to the United States to Milwaukee, Wisconsin, when she was 8 years old, nothing could have suggested that she would later become famous at 71 years old by being appointed Prime Minister of Israel. In this capacity, she is the third woman in the world after Sirimavo Bandaranaike in Sri Lanka and Indira Gandhi in India to ascend to such a governmental position, and the first in Israel. But her international fame, which earned her the nicknames "Iron Lady of Israel", akin to Margaret Thatcher in the United Kingdom, or "the best man in the government" by David Ben-Gurion, founder of Israel, she owes not only to the fact that she is one of the two women who signed the Declaration of Independence of Israel but especially for having led the country during the Israeli-Arab Yom Kippur War in 1973. She was 75 years old at the time and resigned a year later in favor of Yitzhak Rabin. The Yom Kippur War, jointly and surprisingly launched by Egypt and Syria during Ramadan, resulted in more than 2,600 Israeli military casualties and was the cause of the first oil crisis. In 2009, she narrowly escaped an assassination plot organized by the terrorist organization Black September in New York and thwarted by U.S. special services. Golda Meir passed away in 1978 and was buried in Jerusalem.

Joe Biden The U.S. Senate comprises 100 members, with two representing each U.S. state. Who knows them ? Who can name at least five or six without making a mistake, and especially mention from which state they are elected ? Probably not many people outside of the political circles of Washington and accredited journalists specializing in American politics. Indeed, ask around if Donald Trump was a senator before his election as President of the United States, and you will see how widespread ignorance is about this type of institution and its representatives. So let's now turn to Joe Biden, an uninterrupted senator from Delaware for 36 years and unknown to the international public throughout that time, like his other Senate colleagues. Only the voters of Delaware, some of the political, administrative, and economic elite of the United States, knew him more or less well, but certainly not the majority of Americans, let alone the rest of the world. Born in November 1942 in Scranton, Pennsylvania, Joseph Robinette Biden Jr. is originating from a rather affluent family on Long Island, which faced financial difficulties when he was 7 years old, forcing the family to temporarily live with his maternal grandparents, and later to settle in Delaware starting from 1953. Graduate in law from Syracuse University, he practiced law in a firm led by a Democratic activist, which led him to pursue a local political career within the party. He eventually became a senator from Delaware in 1972 by defeating a Republican candidate who was considered a favorite for victory. He thus became one of the youngest individuals elected to such a position. A few weeks later, his wife Neilia and one-year-old daughter Naomi perished in a serious car accident, generating an outpouring of sympathy and compassion from Joe's Delaware constituents from that moment onwards. It's worth noting that tragedy struck Joe Biden again when his son Beau passed away from a brain tumor in 2015. Joe Biden remarried in 1977 to Jill Tracy Jacobs, a teacher he happened to meet. In 1988, Joe Biden attempted to run for the Democratic nomination in the presidential election, but he was forced to withdraw his candidacy amid accusations of plagiarism in some of his speeches and embellishing his CV. In 2008, he made another attempt but failed to surpass Obama and Hillary Clinton. However, Obama was impressed by Biden's campaign style and became convinced that he would make a strong ticket with him for the presidential election. The Democratic convention held in Denver in August 2008 validated this choice, and the rest followed with the election of both men in November 2008, one for the presidency of the United States and Joe Biden for the vice presidency. Joe was then 66 years old and gained national and international prominence by getting involved in hot-button issues such as Afghanistan, Iraq, and Kosovo. In 2012, Barack Obama was re-elected for a second term against Republican Mitt Romney and re-elected Joe Biden as vice president. But it was truly in November 2020, by defeating Donald Trump's bid for a second term, that Joe Biden achieved full international stature by becoming the 46th President of the United States at the age of 78. The controversy surrounding Joe Biden's age and the state of his cognitive faculties has recently escalated in the 2024 presidential campaign. Accumulating gaffes and confusion, at the point of confusing French presidents Mitterrand and Macron or mistaking the president of Egypt for the president of Mexico, a report from special prosecutor Robert Hur highlighted that Joe Biden was an elderly man with a poor memory. This was all the Republican camp needed to relish in, giving Donald Trump the "innocent" opportunity to wonder if Joe Biden remembered that he was still alive. Joe Biden responded in turn, stating, *"I'm well-intentioned, I'm an old man, and I know what I'm doing, darn it ! I don't have a memory problem."* In short, if Joe Biden had not recently decided to hand over to Kamala Harris, voters would have been forced to choose between a "senile" and a "dangerous madman," as political scientist Dominique Moïsi respectively described Joe Biden and Donald Trump. Politics as a means of achieving widespread recognition on both the national and international stage has also served diverse personalities such as François Mitterrand, elected President of the French Republic at 65, François Hollande, virtually unknown at that level until the age of 58 when he became President, or even Donald Trump, who only emerged on the world stage in 2016 at the age of 70 when he became the 45th President of the United States.

WAY NUMBER TWELVE

WAY NUMBER TWELVE : TRAVELING THROUGH TIME

There are several ways to travel through time. One can do so virtually through clairvoyance by attempting to predict the future or through historical research, delving into the past. Or concretely, by using a time machine, although as everyone knows, such a machine does not yet exist and may never exist. Nevertheless, some claim to be a "time traveler," of course remaining silent about how they manage to make successfully this journey. Take the example of the **Count of Saint-Germain**. Regardless of whether the time traveler comes from the past or the future through thought or some undisclosed means, their fame is quickly acquired, even if they are old, or very old. Let's take a few examples : It is difficult to pinpoint the exact birth date of the Count of Saint Germain since historians place it between 1691 and 1712. Genealogical research suggests he was the son of Francis Racoczi, Prince of Transylvania, probably born in 1690. He began to be noticed in European high society from 1742. The Count of Saint Germain was an alchemist, working on the transmutation of lead into gold. French King Louis XV allegedly employed him as a diplomat, Meeting Giacomo Casanova during his travels, Voltaire wrote of him: *"he knows everything and never dies."* It is said of him that he is ageless, that he witnessed the Last Supper and saw Jesus Christ. He speaks dozens of foreign languages, demonstrates a deep knowledge of historical events from any era, and plays music very well. He claims to have lived for hundreds of years thanks to a magical elixir that keeps him eternally young and immortal. Casanova notably says of Saint Germain that he is 300 years old and capable of easily melting diamonds. In 1760, Countess Von Georgy, then an old lady, attends a party hosted by Madame de Pompadour, the mistress of King Louis XV. Introduced to the Count of Saint Germain, she is astonished because she remembers meeting him 50 years earlier in Venice in 1710, when he was courting her. His physical appearance remains the same as she had known it 50 years earlier. She thinks she is meeting his son, but no, the Count assures her that he is indeed the same person she had known, leaving the Countess completely incredulous. He intervenes in a peace treaty during the « Seven Years War » between France and England, then focuses exclusively on alchemy work in Germany, alongside Prince Charles of Hesse- Kassel. The Count of Saint Germain is reported to have died in 1784, but several people claim to have met him years later towards the end of the 18th century.

In 1973, a magician named **Richard Chanfray**, who performs in Parisian theaters, claims to be able to turn lead into gold and that he is in fact the Count of Saint Germain. From a civil status point of view, Chanfray was born in Lyon in 1940 and had a chaotic youth during which, often living on the streets, he committed numerous thefts and even assaulted a woman to rob her. His notoriety in the early 1970s was built on this claim to be

Saint Germain and on the predictions and clairvoyance he gave to famous people. But his fame took on a new dimension when he became the lover and companion of the singer Dalida, whose two previous partners, Lucien Morisse and Luigi Tenco, had committed suicide. Richard Chanfray/Saint Germain claims to be immortal, capable of remembering his past lives, and always able to transmute lead into gold. Chanfray is briefly imprisoned for shooting a naked man he found in his kitchen, who turns out to be only a servant. The man is only slightly injured, but this incident tarnishes Chanfray's reputation, and he separates from Dalida, leading a tumultuous On July 14, 1983, near Saint Tropez, Chanfray/Saint Germain and Paula de Loos committed suicide by ingesting barbiturates and inhaling carbon monoxide in their car. The question then arises : when will the Count of Saint Germain reappear ?

In 1911, Vangeliya Pandeva Dimitrova was born in Bulgaria, better known as **Baba Vanga**. She became blind at the age of 12 due to sand blowing into her eyes during a tornado. She learned Braille at school and how to play the piano. Her first predictions were made in 1927 and only concerned minor local events. In 1939, she recovered from a severe pleurisy against the doctors' prognosis. After turning 30, her predictions broadened, and she attracted clients as a healer and fortune-teller. Among her clients were said to be Tsar Boris III of Bulgaria and even Adolf Hitler. She married a Bulgarian soldier in 1942 and settled in Petrich. After World War II, her clientele expanded to include Bulgarian political leaders from the communist party and beyond, with Leonid Brezhnev, the future leader of the USSR, among them. She claimed to receive her gift of clairvoyance from God. In the 1960s, she worked within the Petrich municipality and a department of the Bulgarian Academy of Sciences, the "Institute of Suggestology," in a role that seems to have been created solely to allow her to exercise her gifts of clairvoyance, especially considering she was almost illiterate. In the 1980s, some of her predictions seemed to concern events that would indeed occur later, such as the sinking of the Russian submarine Kursk in August 2000 or the September 11, 2001 attacks in the United States. Regarding this prediction, she reportedly said, « *horror, horror, the American brothers (an allusion to the Twin Towers of the World Trade Center ?) will fall after being attacked by birds of steel. The wolves will howl in the bush,*» (bush, which led some to say it referred to President George W. Bush in the prediction). She also predicted the death of Princess Diana, the Chernobyl disaster, as well as the election of a black President as the 44th. She also predicted the date of her own death. Her prophecies extend up to 5079, and she predicted the assassination of Vladimir Putin in 2024. It was especially in the 1980s, when she was 70 years old, that her fame spread far beyond the borders of Bulgaria, further reinforced after her death for also predicting the tsunami in Thailand (2004) and the Brexit (2020). She died of breast cancer in 1996, at the age of 85.

One can also gain a certain notoriety later in life by traveling into the past through historical research. This is the case of the French historian **Philippe Ariès**, born in July 1914 in Blois, during the Third Republic. Philippe Ariès, a specialist in medieval history, gained significant attention from the general public starting in 1975 when he published his Essays on the History of Death in the West: From the Middle Ages to the Present Day, followed in 1977 by the book Man Facing Death, and in 1983 Images of Man Facing Death, a year before his own death in February 1984 at the age of 69. These works show, among other things, how death, from being public and accepted in the Middle Ages, became hidden, shameful, and forbidden in our modern societies. Among historians, we can also mention Jean de Joinville, chronicler, and biographer of King Saint Louis. Jean de Joinville, born in Champagne in 1224, joined the court of the King of France Louis IX - future Saint Louis - in 1241 thanks to the intervention of his lord, Thibaud IV of Champagne. Participating in the Seventh Crusade, becoming Counselor to the King, notably during his stay in the Holy Land, Joinville became very close to the king and remained faithful to him until the king's death in Tunis during his last crusade in 1271. Jean de Joinvile became known for writing the Life of Saint Louis, very likely written between 1305 and 1309, when he was already over 80 years old. Louis IX was canonized by the Church in 1297, taking the name Saint Louis, largely thanks to Joinville's testimony, which he delivered in 1282 to ecclesiastical investigators.

WAY NUMBER THIRTEEN

WAY NUMBER THIRTEEN : SURVIVING A WAR, A DISAS-TER, OR A GREAT HUMAN ADVENTURE

Some elderly individuals draw media attention to themselves as soon as they become survivors of a war, a great tragedy, or a particular epic. This was the case with **Claude Bloch**, who passed away at the age of 95 in early January 2024. He was the last survivor of the Auschwitz-Birkenau extermination camp, having been deported there with his mother at the age of 15 in June 1944, and he was on the last convoy of deportees leaving the Drancy camp. His mother was taken to a gas chamber upon arrival at Auschwitz. In May 2023, Claude Bloch participated alongside French President Emmanuel Macron in a commemorative ceremony at Montluc, near Lyon. In addition to the victims of the Holocaust, other individuals have also become famous later in life for bearing witness to other tragedies that have marked world history or for being the last survivor.

Sunao Tsuboi was 20 years old when, on the morning of August 6, 1945, the American super-bomber Enola Gay dropped Little Boy, an atomic bomb, on Hiroshima, a city of 340,000 inhabitants. Sunao, a student engineer, was less than two kilometers from the impact point. The bomb instantly killed tens of thousands of people, and the temperature at the center of the explosion reached around 4000 degrees Celsius for a brief moment. Beyond this instant, it is estimated that this bomb killed between 90,000 and 140,000 people, not counting all those who would later die from cancer due to radiation. In an interview with The New York Times, Mr. Tsuboi said he saw *"a living hell on Earth"* in the moments following the bombing. Sunao was so close to the impact site that he did not see the atomic mushroom cloud at the moment, but only an intense flash of light followed by a loud bang and a blast that threw him into the air. Found alive but unconscious, he was taken to a military hospital covered in burns and wounds. He remained unconscious for 40 days. Having recovered from his injuries, although now suffering from aplastic anemia, Sunao Tsuboi became a math teacher and married a former student in 1957. Every year on August 6, he replaces his classes with a reminder of the horrors of the nuclear bombing and by recounting his own experience. His health is very fragile, and he will be hospitalized 12 times, diagnosed with cancer several times as a result of the radiation he received, and declared terminally ill 3 times by his doctors. In 1993, Mr. Tsuboi retired at the age of 68. Acknowledging that he was not dead when he should have been long ago, he concluded that he was meant to survive to testify that life is above all and that one must fight nuclear weapons, wars, terrorism, and murder. This fight for life and against nuclear weapons received its recognition when Sunao Tsuboi met President Barack Obama in 2016 during his historic visit to Hiroshima, becoming the first American president to do so. During his meeting with Obama, Sunao Tsuboi, then 91 years old, became a symbol of Hiroshima survivors, known as "Hibakusha" in Japanese. Mr. Tsuboi passed away in October 2021 at the age of 96 at Hiroshima Hospital due to heart complications from his anemia.

Léon Gautier was born in Rennes, Brittany, on October 27, 1922. When World War II broke out, he was 16 years old and enlisted in the French navy as a gunner aboard the Courbet. He took part in the defense of the port of Cherbourg. In June 1940, the Courbet joined the Free French Forces in England and participated in the anti-aircraft defense of Portsmouth. In July, he was aboard a merchant ship, "Le Gallois," which was sunk by a German U-Boat in the Atlantic. He witnessed his fellow sailors, like himself, abandoned by other ships ordered not to stop, fearing they would be sunk too. This episode, from which he emerged alive, marked him deeply. In January 1941, Léon Gautier embarked on the Surcouf, a French submarine, and served as a marine rifleman in various missions in Cameroon, Lebanon, and Syria. He joined the commandos after training in Scotland and became part of the first Marine Commando Battalion led by Commander Philippe Kieffer. In 1943, he coincidentally met his future wife Dorothy during one of his guard duties. She was wounded in the head by shrapnel in 1943 in Calais, but this did not prevent Léon Gautier from marrying her some time later. On June 6, 1944, D-Day in Normandy, Léon Gautier and the other members of the 1st Battalion of Marine Fusilier Commandos led by Lieutenant-Colonel Philippe Kieffer were in the onto the barges landing at Sword Beach in Normandy. After successfully breaching the German artillery defense, the commando seized the Riva Bella casino in Ouistreham, then successfully joined forces with the British airborne troops of the 6th Airborne Division to seize their main objective, the Pegasus Bridge in Bénouville. On the evening of June 6, the Kieffer battalion had lost a quarter of its troops in the day's fighting, with Commander Kieffer himself among the wounded. Subsequently, Léon Gautier and the other commando members would engage in combat in Normandy for 78 days before returning to England due to an ankle injury. Returning to civilian life after the war, he worked in a workshop in England, joined the French Company of West Africa, and worked notably in Cameroon and Biafra. Upon his return to France, he resumed studying law, became an automotive expert, and led a discreet life for many years. With his family, starting in 1982, he was involved in the creation of a Norman museum dedicated to the action of the Kieffer commandos in Ouistreham, and he participated in all commemorative ceremonies until the 70th anniversary of D-Day on June 6, 2014, when the spotlight shone on him. He then embraced his German friend Johannes Börner, a paratrooper captured in the Falaise Pocket, in front of a gathering of Heads of State, including US President Barack Obama, French President François Hollande, and the Queen of England. He was made a Commander of the Legion of Honor in August 2016 and received his distinction from the French Prime Minister. Léon Gautier was also a member of the Order of the British Empire, holder of the Military Medal, the Croix de Guerre 1939-1945, the Resistance Medal, and the Cross of Volunteer Combatants. He passed away at the age of 100 in July 2023 from a lung infection, becoming the last survivor of the 177 French soldiers to land in Normandy. Upon his death, President Macron paid tribute to him and his brothers in arms, highlighting their virtues as fighters and men of peace, and expressing the nation's eternal gratitude.

Elizabeth Gladys "Millvina" Dean would never have any memory of that day, April 10, 1912, when she embarked from Southampton. On a cruise ship bound for New York with her parents. And for good reason, she was just two months old! The name of the ship? RMS Titanic. Millvina's parents lived in London and wished to immigrate to Wichita, Kansas, hoping to operate a tobacco shop there. Initially, the Deans had booked their passage on a less luxurious White Star ship, the Adriatic, but a coal strike affecting delivery had forced the White Star Line to transfer their reservation to the much more prestigious Titanic, but only in third class. The rest is known to all regarding the Titanic. On the night of April 14, 1912, the Titanic struck an iceberg in the North Atlantic and sank two hours later. The disaster would claim 1500 lives and spare 705. Among the survivors were Millvina, her mother, and her younger brother, just two years her junior. Among the victims was Millvina's father, only 25 years old. Millvina's mother and her two young children, aboard lifeboat number 10, were among the first passengers from the ship's steerage to evacuate and subsequently board the Carpathia, which came to the Titanic's rescue. They safely disembarked in New York on April 18. Widowed and responsible for two young children, Millvina's mother abandoned plans to settle in the United States and returned to England two weeks later after leaving the hospital. On the return ship, the Adriatic, Millvina, the youngest survivor of the disaster, was the center of attention among passengers, as reported in a Daily Mirror article dated May 12, 1912. It wasn't until she was 8 years old that Millvina became aware she was a Titanic survivor. She was educated with the support of charitable organizations. Later, she would work for the British Government during World War II and then in a purchasing department of an engineering company until her retirement in 1972. Throughout this time, she attended all events related to or commemorating the history and tragedy of the Titanic. In 1997, she was invited to make a transatlantic crossing on the Queen Elizabeth II and she accepted despite the Titanic's precedent. That same year, James Cameron's film Titanic, starring Leonardo DiCaprio and Kate Winslet and featuring music by James Horner, was released, which was a huge success and received numerous awards. With multiple awards, including 14 Academy Award nominations, the film brought renewed attention to this 85-year-old woman, the youngest survivor of the disaster. However, given that she had lost her father in the shipwreck, Millvina chose not to watch the film in its entirety. Millvina, who passed away in May 2009, became the last survivor of the Titanic sinking, following the death in 2006 of Lillian Gertrud Asplund, the last American survivor of the Titanic. Surprisingly, Millvina Dean passed away at the age of 98 on May 31, coincidentally the same date the Titanic's hull was launched 98 years earlier. Ultimately, Millvina Dean is remembered for being both the youngest survivor and the oldest survivor of this tragedy.

To conclude this chapter on the last survivors, we must also mention **Lazare Ponticelli**, an Italian immigrant in France who was 16 when World War I broke out. Enlisting in the Foreign Legion in gratitude to his adopted country, he was among the 8.5 million soldiers who served in the Great War. Being the last surviving poilu (French soldier of World War I) and the dean of the legionnaires, Lazare Ponticelli received a national funeral at Les Invalides in Paris on March 17, 2008, attended by Nicolas Sarkozy, President of the French Republic, Jacques Chirac, former President, and the Italian Minister of Defense. Ponticelli had agreed before his death to receive a national funeral not for himself but in memory of all the others. While not the last survivor of a war or disaster, one may also have embarked on a remarkable human adventure later in life.

Such is the case of **Carlos Soria Fontan**, a Spaniard born in 1939, who inscribes himself in the long history of world mountaineering. His first Himalayan expedition was in 1990 at the age of 51, when he ascended Nanga Parbat (8,125m). Born the son of a carpet maker, he fell in love with the mountains at the age of

14. However, his most significant achievements all came after the age of 60. Consider this : Everest (8,849m) at 62, K2 (8,611m) at 65, Makalu (8,465m) at 69, Lhotse (8,516m) at 72, Kangchenjunga (8,586m) at 75, Annapurna (8,091m) at 77. By 2023, he had already conquered twelve of the fourteen peaks over 8,000 meters and had recently had to abandon his thirteenth attempt to climb Dhaulagiri (8,167m), just 700 meters from the summit due to a leg fracture sustained from a fall. At the age of 84, one of the Nepalese guides in his team died, a rather ironic twist. In December 2000, when Carlos Soria bought a car, the number plate coincided with the height of Everest (8,848m). Tribute must also be paid in this section to **Marcel Rémy,** a Swiss who passed away at the age of 99 in 2022. He had still climbed the "miroir d'Argentine" in 2017, a vertical limestone wall of 450 meters in the Vaudois Alps, well into his 94th year.

WAY NUMBER FOURTEEN

WAY NUMBER FOURTEEN : HAVING A LOUD VOICE, OR-
ATORICAL TALENT, AND BEING INTIMIDATING

When you earn the nickname "The Tiger", it's not because you're particularly likable but rather because you're fierce with your enemies. Born in 1841 in Vendée, a rebellious land against revolutionary ideas, into a family of doctors, **Georges Benjamin Clemenceau** had a relatively comfortable youth in a rural area, poor and distant from Paris. Especially since his father, instead of practicing medicine, contented himself with living off his land and investments. He was a Voltairian, an admirer of the French Revolution, and a critic of Napoleon III, whom he dreamed of seeing overthrown. Clemenceau's youth unfolded under the Second Empire, which he did not hold in high regard. He left his native Vendée to study medicine first in Nantes and then in Paris. After a brief stay in America to recover from a love disappointment, he eventually married an American woman with whom he resettled in Vendée in 1869. At the age of twenty, Clemenceau frequented republican circles in Paris thanks to his father's connections and began to frequent the literary cafes of the Latin Quarter while attacking the supporters of the Second Empire and its political regime. He was notably a member of a small association called Agis Comme Tu Penses (Act as You Think), which attracted trouble with the imperial police. Wanting to commemorate the 14th anniversary of the 1848 revolution with his comrades, Georges Clemenceau was arrested and spent 73 days in prison. He then went to the United States, particularly New York, while the CivilWar was raging. Seduced by the freedom of expression of American politicians, he taught at a girls' school in Stamford and eventually married one of them, Mary Plummer. Returning to France, he quickly resumed his political activities, witnessing Napoleon III declare war on Germany in July 1870 and his army collapse at Sedan two months later. He was elected Mayor of the XVIIIth arrondissement of Paris. Léon Gambetta and the republican deputies declared the emperor's deposition and proclaimed the Republic in September 1870. Following the defeat against the Prussians, Adolphe Thiers, a former minister of Louis-Philippe, became head of the executive power in February 1871. Georges Clemenceau founded La Justice, a newspaper favorable to extreme left-wing ideas, which quickly became the leading organ of this political tendency. Like all the deputies of Paris, he opposed France's ratification of the armistice convention in March 1871, which provided for the cession of Alsace-Lorraine territories to Germany. He became involved in the insurrection of the Paris Commune, which was brutally suppressed by the Versailles troops under the auspices of Adolphe Thiers. Georges Clemenceau thundered and raged in his newspaper against the government and its ministers, against colonization policies, against Georges Boulanger when he turned out to be nothing but a nationalist demagogue, against the trafficking of decorations during the time of Jules Grévy. Georges Clemenceau ruined many ministerial careers with his outbursts and polemical talent, earning him many enemies who would try to take revenge when Georges Clemenceau was implicated in the Panama Canal scandal through his association with the financier Cornelius Herz, who was himself heavily implicated. Paul Déroulède, a Boulangist supporter, accused Georges Clemenceau of corruption in the Panama Canal affair, as well as of being paid by the British government for delivering Egypt to the English. This was too much for Clemenceau, who published an inflammatory article against Déroulède in his newspaper La Justice. Given his refusal to withdraw the article at Déroulède's request, a sword duel became inevitable and took place in July 1894. The duel did not kill anyone and only slightly injured Déroulède in the forehead. Clemenceau proved to be a fan of duels, as he also fought, this time with pistols, against the journalist Edouard Drumont in February 1898 regarding the Dreyfus affair. Already in 1865, when he came to support his friend Manet at an exhibition where Manet's painting Olympia caused a scandal, Clemenceau attacked a detractor, slapped him, and then challenged him to a duel. Clemenceau was also an indefatigable womanizer. Having divorced, he frequented all the literary and musical salons of the Belle Époque and seduced dancers from the Paris Opera, actresses, singers, and demimondaines. It was in his sixties that Georges Clemenceau would propel his political career during the Dreyfus affair, which saw this French Army Jewish officer accused of treason in favor of the Germans. Convinced of his innocence, Clemenceau fought for his cause in La Justice and L'Aurore, which also earned him a seat as senator in Var in 1902. He was the one who gave the famous title "J'accuse" (I accuse) to Emile Zola's diatribe against the French General Staff in L'Aurore. He also fought for the abolition of the death penalty. In 1906, he was appointed Minister of the Interior, then Prime Minister. He modernized the police force and created the famous "brigades du Tigre" (the Tiger brigades), equipping policemen with the first automobiles and effective firearms. His cabinet fell in 1909, and he returned to journalism and advocated for military strengthening against Germany. From 1917, Clemenceau, then President of the Council and Minister of War, led France to victory by imposing the union of the Allied armies under the single command of Marshal Foch and negotiated the Treaty of Versailles. He was then 76 years old. His authority was unquestioned, and his determination was known to all. Georges Clemenceau had now entered history. "The Tiger", a nickname partly based on his reputation as a strikebreaker and chief of police, became "Father of Victory". In 1920, Deschanel took his revenge by surpassing him in the presidential election. Clemenceau then retired from politics and died in 1929 at the age of 88. Of course, Clemenceau could have been included in medium number eleven, "engaging in politics," or sixteen, "becoming a great war leader," but I chose to include him in this chapter on "great voices" because it was his personality, made of natural authority, tireless combativeness, unwavering determination, oratorical talent, and journalism, that truly built Clemenceau's career and reputation.

Donald John Trump, nicknamed "The Donald," was born in June 1946 in New York City, in the Queens borough, to a real estate developer father, Fred Trump, and his Scottish wife, Mary Anne. He has two brothers and two sisters. His older brother, Freddy, died young at the age of 43 from alcoholism in 1981. Donald's father built hundreds of housing units in Queens and Brooklyn using federal loans intended for social housing construction. He would later be accused of overcharging construction costs to exploit the federally guaranteed loan system. Donald Trump attended the New York Military Academy from 1959 to 1964 and then, after a stint at a university in the Bronx, earned a Bachelor's degree in Economics from the Wharton School of Finance and Commerce at the University of Pennsylvania. During the VietnamWar in 1968, he managed to obtain a medical deferment, claiming a bone spur in his heel, even though at 22 he seemed to be in excellent health, regularly playing football, tennis, squash, and golf. He later claimed that it was the draft lottery of the National Conscription Bureau that allowed him to be exempted, which turned out to be false. He then began working for his father in real estate, with his father managing a housing portfolio of between 10,000 and 20,000 units. During the 1960s and early 1970s, both he and his father faced complaints of racial discrimination in their choice of tenants. They would eventually be sued by the U.S. Department of Justice in 1973 for real estate operations in New York City. In 1974, he took over the Trump Organization, and by the late 1980s, Donald Trump had greatly expanded his father's business by investing in luxury hotels, residential buildings, and casinos in Manhattan, Atlantic City, and New Jersey. In 1983, he opened the Trump Tower, a 58-story building on Fifth Avenue in New York, which houses the headquarters of the Trump Organization. In Atlantic City, his properties include the Harrah's casino in the Trump Plaza, the Trump's Castle Casino Resort, and the Trump Taj Mahal, one of the world's largest casinos. He purchased the Mar-a-Lago estate in Florida, a 118-room mansion, and owns a nearly 90-meter-long yacht, the Trump Princess. He is also responsible for the construction of the Jacob Javits Convention Center in western Manhattan and the renovation of Grand Central Terminal. Donald Trump's real estate operations are numerous, not only in the United States but also abroad, such as his acquisitions of golf clubs in Scotland or Ireland. Donald Trump's private life has been quite tumultuous. In 1977, he married Ivana Zelníčkova Winklmayr, a Czech top model, with whom he had three children, including his daughter Ivanka. They divorced in 1992, and his romantic escapades delighted the tabloid press. He then remarried Marla Maples, with whom he had a daughter, Tiffany, in 1993. They divorced again in 1999, and he remarried in 2005 to Slovenian-born model Melania Knavs, who is 24 years his junior. Their son, Barron, was born in 2006. In the early 1990s, Donald Trump's businesses suffered due to the economic recession affecting the country at the time, and his personal fortune significantly decreased, forcing him to sell casinos and his yacht to pay off debts. He regained financial health from the late 1990s onwards, thanks to lines of credit opened to him by Deutsche Bank AG. In 1996, he partnered with NBC to purchase the Miss Universe Organization, which oversees beauty pageants such as Miss USA and Miss Teen USA. In the mid-2000s, as Donald Trump reached his sixties, his reality TV show The Apprentice became a phenomenal success, earning him over $200 million and catapulting his fame as a successful billionaire. The premise of the show is to allow participants to compete for a one-year job contract within one of Donald Trump's organizations. In this show, which always features very attractive women, Donald Trump acts as the master of ceremonies and ruthless businessman, becoming famous for his catchphrase *"You're fired"*, directed at the unlucky contestants of this reality TV game. The only way to win is to impress the boss, Donald Trump himself. The show takes place in the Trump Tower in Manhattan. There are two elevators : one goes to the top for those who pass the test successfully, while the other goes directly to the street for those who are fired by Trump. Donald Trump's remarks are numerous. He invents words, ridicules his opponents, and displays hostility towards certain communities, referring to "Blacks," "Gays," and "Muslims." Some of his remarks are openly racist, such as when he advised four Democratic congresswomen of minority backgrounds to "go back" to their countries of origin, despite all four being American citizens. Delicacy is not his strong suit. In the midst of the 2016 presidential campaign, Donald Trump attempts to take down his rival Hillary Clinton by recalling the escapades of her husband Bill Clinton with Monica Lewinsky. He declares: *"The worst thing Hillary could do is have her husband campaigning with her."* Donald Trump has a habit of giving humorous or derogatory nicknames to his opponents ; Hillary Clinton becomes "Crooked Hillary", Chuck Schumer, a senator, becomes "Cryin' Chuck", Joe Biden is nicknamed "Sleepy Creepy Joe", and Kamala Harris, the Democratic Vice President, is referred to in Trumpian language as "Nasty Kamala." A Native American senator, Elizabeth Warren, is nicknamed Pocahontas. Sexist remarks are also numerous. In 2005, Donald Trump made comments like: *"When you're a star, they let you do it. You can do anything. Grab 'em by the pussy."* In 2015, he stated, *"If Hillary Clinton can't satisfy her husband, how can she satisfy the country ?"* Even worse, regarding his own daughter Ivanka: *"If Ivanka weren't my daughter, perhaps I'd be dating her."* In his last Christmas message in 2023, Donald Trump wishes his political opponents, whom he calls thugs or crooks, to all rot in hell. The repeated provocations, colorful language, outbursts, and bluffs, along with Donald Trump's false allegations, garnered him popularity and media coverage within the United States. This led him to become the Republican candidate in the 2016 primary elections against the Democratic camp led by Hillary Clinton. During the debates between the two candidates, Trump even went as far as refusing to say whether he would accept the election result. Donald "the loudmouth" became an international celebrity in November 2016 when he was elected the 45th President of the United States, the first president to have neither served in the military nor held a government position before. Donald Trump was then 70 years old. In 2019, the first impeachment proceedings were launched by the Speaker of the House of Representatives, Nancy Pelosi, on the grounds that Donald Trump pressured Ukrainian President Volodymyr Zelensky to investigate the foreign dealings of Joe Biden's son, Hunter Biden. In 2020, the Senate thwarted this initiative. In 2020, Donald Trump attempted to run for re-election but was defeated by Joe Biden, contesting the results up to the Capitol incident. Donald Trump will refuse to participate in Joe Biden's inauguration and will not acknowledge his electoral defeat. 30 On July 13, 2024, Donald Trump narrowly escaped an assassination attempt near Butler in Pennsylvania and was apparently targeted by another one in September 2024 as he golfed near his Florida club. In November 2024, Donald Trump won the presidential election, making a resounding comeback! He is now in charge of his country for 4 years more at the age of 78, while having become, over the course of his eventful life, a real character from a novel.

Jean Luc Mélenchon was born in Tangier, Morocco, on August 19, 1951, into a family of pied-noirs from Algeria with Spanish and Italian (Sicilian) ancestry. His father was a postman, and his mother was a teacher. He received a religious education and even served as an altar boy for a time. His parents divorced in 1962, which gave his mother the opportunity to move to France, first to Normandy in the Caux region, then to the Jura. He attended high school in Lons-le-Saunier at the Rouget de Lisle high school and obtained his baccalaureate in 1969. He then enrolled at the University of Franche-Comté in Besançon, where he earned a degree in philosophy and a degree in modern literature. In his youth, he was active in the National Union of French Students (Unef) and the Internationalist Communist Organization, a Trotskyist and Lambertist group. He notably participated in the struggles of the workers at the Lip watchmaking company in Besançon and in student support collectives. He began working in blue-collar jobs and then started a career in the national education system as a supervisor and substitute teacher. With a CAPES (teaching qualification) in modern literature, he was appointed a French teacher at a high school in the Jura region. A member of the Socialist Party from 1977 to 2008, thanks to the support of Claude Germon, then mayor of Massy Palaiseau, he settled in Essonne and eventually held elected positions as municipal councilor of Massy Palaiseau in 1983, then general councilor of Essonne in 1985, and finally senator for the same department in 1986. Throughout this journey, he contributed to various publications of the Socialist Party. At the Socialist Party Congress in Valence in 1981, when François Mitterrand was leading the party, just before his election as President of the French Republic, Jean-Luc Mélenchon took control of the Socialist Federation of Essonne as the first secretary. He fought locally in this area until 1986 and even founded a local radio station. In 1992, he called for a vote in favor of the Maastricht Treaty, convinced that the single currency, the euro, would allow Europe to free itself from the financial control of the US dollar. Later, he completely changed his mind and asserted that Maastricht was a total failure. In 1997, during the Congress in Brest, he ran for the position of first secretary of the Socialist Party against François Hollande and suffered a crushing defeat. From then on, he continuously acted as a maverick within the Socialist Party, particularly against the followers of Hollande. In March 2000, while there was a cohabitation between President Jacques Chirac and Socialist Prime Minister Lionel Jospin, Jean Luc Mélenchon accepted a government position as Minister Delegate for Vocational Education, under the Minister of National Education, Jack Lang. Lionel Jospin's defeat in the 2002 presidential election relegated Jean Luc Mélenchon to the role of a political agitator on the far left of the Socialist Party and to relative anonymity. In 2008, after Nicolas Sarkozy was elected President of the French Republic, defeating Ségolène Royal, the Socialist Party's candidate in 2007, he resigned from the Socialist Party and founded the Left Party, which later evolved into La France Insoumise (LFI). In the 2009 European elections, he became a Member of the European Parliament, representing a constituency in the Southwest, and began to assert himself on the media and political scene through his relentless diatribes against the ruling class and its administrative elites. In a book published in 2010 titled "They Must All Go!", he criticizes many bosses, liberal or right-wing politicians, and journalists loyal to these ideological currents, labeling them as profiteers and parasites. The book was quite successful and allowed Mélenchon to hammer home the idea of "corrupt elites" and praise the left-wing revolutions in Latin America. Mélenchon demonizes, vituperates, uses animalistic language, caricatures his opponents, appeals to emotional impulses and fears, and invokes the language of diseases (cancer of finance, virus of the far right contaminating leaders, etc.). For him, money is always stolen from the people for the benefit of those who gorge themselves. He is unafraid of populist discourse and readily rebuffs his opponents with sharp retorts, inciting fear with his anger, whether genuine or assumed. During a police raid in 2018 on the premises of his party La France Insoumise, following an investigation into his campaign accounts and the employment of parliamentary assistants, he displayed acts of intimidation, rebellion, and provocation towards the police, declaring in a lyrical outburst : *The Republic is me !"* At that time, Jean Luc Mélenchon was 67 years old, and his national notoriety was significant. From then on, the electoral machinery is launched. In the 2012 presidential elections, he ran as the leader of the Left Front and garnered over 11% of the votes, placing fourth behind François Hollande, Nicolas Sarkozy, Marine Le Pen, and ahead of François Bayrou. He then contested in the Pas-de-Calais in the subsequent legislative elections, was defeated, and henceforth opposed the Hollande presidency, for which he did not explicitly endorse in 2012, merely calling to block Nicolas Sarkozy's path. From then on, he was present at all demonstrations, appeared on morning news programs on TV channels, criticized electoral agreements with some of his partners, such as the Communist Party, the Socialist Party, or the Greens, while trying to unite them under his leadership. In 2017, he ran for president again based on flattering poll numbers and the support of his new movement La France Insoumise (France Unbowed). He was by far one of the best speakers in the political class at the time and was not hesitant to innovate by using digital technologies (hologram) suggested by his young communication director and partner, Sophia Chikirou. The campaign was a success, and within a few weeks, his support increased from 11% to 19% in the polls. From then on, he became the target of attacks. His program was deemed delusional, he was labeled as an apostle of revolutionary dictators, as irresponsible; some considered that he used the same populist methods as the far-right. But the smell of gunpowder did not displease Jean Luc Mélenchon, who once again finished fourth, just behind the third-placed François Fillon and behind Emmanuel Macron and Marine Le Pen. In the subsequent legislative elections, he was elected as a deputy for Bouches-du-Rhône in Marseille, not without accusing the former Prime Minister Bernard Cazeneuve of *"dealing with the assassination of Rémi Fraisse,"* an environmental activist killed by a gendarme grenade in 2014. This led to defamation charges against him. In 2022, Mélenchon ran for president for the third time, reused digital technologies, including olfactory ones, and this time finished third, very narrowly behind Marine Le Pen and probably because this time his partnership with the Communist Party broke down. In the subsequent legislative elections, he asked the French to *"elect him as Prime Minister,"* established the New Popular Ecological and Social Union (NUPES), while not being a candidate for deputy himself. The NUPES was an electoral success at least until October 2023, when the Socialist Party had vote for a moratorium on his participation in the activities of this union, questioning "the Mélenchon method". For the 2027 presidential elections, Jean Luc Mélenchon stated, *"circumstances dictate candidacies"*. He will be 76 years old. He probably excludes nothing. If he succeeds, his fame will instantly become very widespread on the international stage. Recently, on the occasion of the criticism of the jewish journalist Ruth Elkrief, who was called a fanatic by Mélenchon, the psychoanalyst Gérard Miller, although a fellow traveler of La France Insoumise, stated, *"It is obvious that the noise and fury, which were at one point quite fruitful in the history of Mélenchonism, are now deafening"*. The paradox is also the fact that Gérard Miller, 76 years old, is now in turn generating noise and fury due to dozens of accusations of rape and sexual assault currently leveled against him. The President of the French Senate, Gérard Larcher, subsequently added fuel to the fire by advising Jean Luc Mélenchon to "shut his mouth" following the latest controversies surrounding journalist Ruth Elkrief.

On June 20, 1928, in La Trinité-sur-Mer, in Morbihan (France), was born from the love of a fisherman and a seamstress, **Jean Louis Marie Le Pen**. He was an only child. Pen means "chief" in Breton language. At the age of 14, in August 1942, he lost his father when his trawler hit a mine while hauling its nets. His father, declared "Mort pour la France" (Died for France), became a ward of the state by a judgment of the civil court of Lorient. He initially studied with the Jesuits at Saint-François Xavier College in Vannes and at Dupuy-de-Lôme High School in Lorient. He was expelled several times for indiscipline. Then he tried to join the Free French Forces in November 1944 but was rejected because he was not yet 18 years old and a ward of the state. With his baccalaureate in hand, he joined the Faculty of Law in Paris in 1948 and obtained a bachelor's degree. In 1949, thanks to his already evident oratory skills, he was elected president of the Corporate Association of Law Students, the "Corpo" of law. During his studies, which he financed by taking various odd jobs (coal miner, apartment measurer, etc.), he felt close to the Action Française and had to relinquish the presidency of the Corpo in 1952 under criticism for his numerous verbal and even physical excesses. Indeed, during this period, he was known for getting into fistfights with "the Reds" and for indulging in drunken nocturnal escapades in bars, which often landed him in the police station and led to him sometimes getting convicted of assault and battery. With his law degree in hand, he enlisted in the first parachute regiment of the French Foreign Legion and campaigned in Algeria and Indochina from 1953 to 1957, which would later give rise to various controversies about whether Jean-Marie Le Pen had practiced torture during the Algerian War. In an interview with the newspaper Combat in November 1962, he said, *"I tortured because it had to be done. When someone is brought to you who has just planted twenty bombs that could explode at any moment and he refuses to talk, you have to use exceptional means to compel him."* Regardless, Jean-Marie Le Pen was decorated several times for his exploits, receiving notably the Croix de la Valeur Militaire (Cross of Military Valour), the Colonial Medal, and various commemorative medals for his campaigns in Algeria and the Far East. Upon his return from Indochina, he became the general delegate of the Union of French Youth Defense, was introduced to Pierre Poujade, a populist politician defending traders and artisans, and in the Poujadist electoral wave, he became, at 27, one of the youngest deputies of the legislature, elected in the first constituency of the Seine. At the end of this term, he directed the campaign of the farright lawyer Jean-Louis Tixier-Vignancour, and he was re-elected as a deputy in 1958 in his former constituency. Later, he would explain that he lost an eye while setting up the tent for a rightwing extremist Tixier-Vignancour rally, although some claim that it was as a result of an electoral brawl that he gradually lost the use of that eye. In any case, he wore an eyepatch for a while, giving him more the look of a Caribbean pirate than that of a university professor or a clergyman. In 1958, he confronted Pierre Mendès France, former Prime Minister, who was Jewish, in these terms: *"Mr. Mendès France, your character crystallizes a certain number of patriotic, almost physical repulsions. "* Even if he later denies it, pretending only to find him very ugly, without his Jewishness being taken into account, it is certainly a manifestation that can be described as anti-Semitic. During the insurrection of the supporters of French Algeria, he clearly sided with the insurgents, associated with members of the OAS, a far-right terrorist organization, and former collaborators of the Nazi regime, such as Darquier de Pellepoix, Léon Degrelle, not even former Nazis like Otto Skorzeny. From 1963 onwards, his commitment to the far-right never wavered. Subsequently, after supporting Jean-Louis Tixier Vignancour's candidacy in 1965, he later joined the leaders of the Ordre Nouveau movement, an organization within the Neo-fascist movement, which participated in the creation of the National Front in 1972. Jean-Marie Le Pen's private life mirrors his public life, often tumultuous, sometimes scandalous, punctuated by episodes that delight the tabloid press. After his tumultuous youth, he married at the age of 32 with Pierrette Lalanne, daughter of a wine merchant from Landes and ex-wife of an impresario who would introduce her to Jean-Marie Le Pen by saying, *"You'll see, he's the future dictator of France."* Pierrette was pregnant with Jean-Marie's child even before officially divorcing her impresario husband. A daughter, Marie Caroline, was born in January 1960. Two more children, Yann and Marine, followed. The couple separated in 1972 amid acrimony. *"You'll come back to Saint-Cloud (the couple's residence) on your knees, I'll put you in the cellar and I'll pee on your head,"* Jean-Marie reportedly said to Perrette, according to her statements to the Globe newspaper. When Perrette, now destitute, sought shelter with friends, Jean-Marie Le Pen declared, *"It's an opportunity for her to make use of that little beautician diploma she got in the 1960s. Otherwise, she can do some cleaning to supplement her in-*

come." Pierrette was of the playmate type, not hesitating to expose her body quite extensively, including later in 1987 in the men's magazine Playboy, partly to get back at Jean-Marie Le Pen, appearing naked with just a maid outfit, her way of doing housework! According to an article published in Les Inrockuptibles in 2011, the family vaguely reconciled around the three daughters, although in the meantime Jean-Marie Le Pen had started a new life with another woman, Jany, daughter of a Greek art dealer. The episode tarnished the image of the good family man that Jean-Marie was trying to build for political communication reasons with his electorate. Especially since in 1976, a 20kg bomb exploded in the Poirier villa in the XVth arrondissement of Paris, where the couple and their three daughters lived. The attack, never claimed or elucidated, fortunately caused no victims but contributed to spreading fear. The controversies surrounding the charismatic leader of the National Front are manifold. His tumultuous private life, contrary to the values of Jean- Marie Le Pen's traditionalist electorate, nonetheless reflects quite well his usual behavior, which is often seen as macho, sexist, and libertarian. His daughter Marine reportedly once said, *"My father is against policing underwear."* Another issue that sparked controversy is how he inherited a significant real estate portfolio from Hubert Lambert, who died at 42 from liver cirrhosis with no direct heirs. Lambert had amassed his fortune from his parents who owned Lambert Cement, a construction materials company. The inheritance, valued at 30 million francs, included a mansion in the Montretout park in Saint-Cloud. The will was contested by the deceased's cousin, claiming that Jean-Marie Le Pen had taken advantage of Hubert Lambert's alcoholism and mental impairment to become a beneficiary in the will. Eventually, the matter was settled amicably between the parties, but it left doubts about Jean-Marie Le Pen's behavior. Jean-Marie Le Pen's verbal slips are countless, ranging from questionable to outright condemnable.

In September 1987, he stated on RTL that gas chambers were *"a detail of history."* In 1988, he made a very questionable pun on the name of Michel Durafour, then Minister of Public Service, calling him *"Monsieur Durafour crematorium."* In May 1997, he verbally attacked the socialist mayor of Mantes-la-Jolie, shouting at her while she, rather frail, protected herself with her hands as she was cornered against a wall. During the same visit, he called a protester a "fag" and punched and kicked another socialist elected official. In 2005, he stated in the far-right newspaper Rivarol that *"the German occupation in France was not particularly inhumane."* In 2014, he targeted artists who spoke out against his party, including singer Patrick Bruel, who is Jewish. *"Listen, we'll do a batch next time."* These remarks led to him being brought to court for incitement to racial hatred. Also in the same year, he claimed that the Ebola virus could solve the immigration problem in three months. During the regional elections of 2015, commenting on one of his tweets mocking Christian Estrosi, major of Nice, dancing with Jews, he stated, refuting any antisemitic implication, *"We found it funny to show Christian Estrosi laughing and dancing when he had just been kicked in the butt."* All these statements and actions earned him several convictions by the Justice system for antisemitism. But it's truly in April 2002, when Jean-Marie Le Pen is 74 years old, that his fame will literally cross national borders when, to everyone's surprise, he reaches the second round of the presidential election with Jacques Chirac, eliminating Lionel Jospin, who until then seemed widely favored for the election. In September 2024, aged 96, he was filmed singing with a neo- Nazi rock band in the city of Lyon.

WAY NUMBER FIFTEEN

WAY NUMBER FIFTEEN : DEFYING NATURAL LAWS

A certain number of elderly individuals, previously unknown, gain fame late in life by defying natural laws in one way or another that govern us. **Paul Richard Alexander** recently made headlines by passing away on March 11, 2024, at the age of 78. Born in Dallas, Texas, in January 1946, to immigrant parents, he contracted polio in 1952 at the age of six during an epidemic that hit North America, leaving 21,000 people paralyzed in the United States alone. For Paul, the resulting paralysis left him with only the freedom to move his neck, head, and mouth. He was placed in an iron lung, the only way to keep him alive, but doctors suggested to his parents that he wouldn't survive long. After a year and a half in the hospital, where, during power outages, the device had to be manually operated, he managed to learn a breathing technique that allowed him to occasionally do without the apparatus for a few hours. This allowed him to pursue secondary and university education, relying entirely on his memory since he could not use his hands. He took courses in finance and economics, eventually graduating in law from the University of Texas at Austin in 1984 at the age of 38. He wrote a book titled Three Minutes for a Dog: My Life in an Iron Lung, and later opened a TikTok account that gathered over 330,000 followers, where he recounted his existence in the iron lung and shared life lessons. In 2022, Paul told CNN that he was working on writing a second book. In March 2023, the Guinness World Records declared Alexander to be the person who spent the most time in an iron lung, a total of 70 years. Upon the announcement of his death, his brother Philip stated, *"It's absolutely incredible to read all the comments and know that so many people have been inspired by Paul's life."*

Charlie Bancarel, a former bus driver, had his moment of glory in April 2023 when he completed the Paris Marathon at the age of 93 in 7 hours and 22 minutes. Charlie, who ran his first marathon at 70, made headlines again at the 2024 Olympic Games marathon, held in Paris. Charlie ran in good company during the 2023 marathon as he was accompanied by **Barbara Humbert**, 83, who finished the race an hour faster than him. The privilege of youth ? In 2020, at the height of the COVID-19 epidemic, the spaniard **Ana del Valle** was honored by the press for having survived both the Spanish flu epidemic of 1918, which claimed between 50 and 100 million lives worldwide, and the COVID-19 pandemic, at the age of 106 and unvaccinated. It is worth noting that Spain was the European country most affected by the virus, recording over 22,000 deaths. James Hiram Bedford only became famous upon his death on January 12, 1967, at the age of 73.

James Hiram Bedford was a psychology professor and career development specialist in San Joaquin Valley, California. His first wife, Anna Chandler Rice, passed away the same year they married, and James remarried three years later in 1920 to Ruby McLagan, with whom he had five children. In 1965, when James, born in April 1893, was 72 years old, the Ev Cooper's Life Extension Society (LES) offered the opportunity for a volunteer to be the first to undergo cryopreservation for free. The LES was founded in 1964 by Evan Cooper, who two years earlier had published an article under a pseudonym titled *Immortality: Physically, Scientifically, Now*. The general idea of the article is that humans are not condemned to die once born, but rather it is possible to freeze them shortly before death and give them a chance to live again, healthy and whole, forever. At the same time, a physics professor in Michigan, Robert Ettinger, developed a similar idea in a book titled The Prospect of Immortality, which gained more attention than Cooper's article because it received a recommendation from the famous science-fiction writer Isaac Asimov (author of the Galactic Empire) and another author known for his Sci-Fi stories, Fred Pohl. Nevertheless, the credit for creating the first cryogenic societies and facilities unquestionably belongs to Evan Cooper. While the Life Extension Society ceased its activities at the end of the 1960s, the activity was revived in 1992 in Maryland. Regarding James Hiram Bedford, he was suffering from metastatic kidney cancer that had spread to his lungs and had no prospect of survival with the treatments available in the mid-1960s. James took the initiative and contacted several doctors who were members of the cryonics society at different times. They explained that they would have only seven minutes from the moment of death to perform the cryonic procedure. The fateful day came soon after the grim diagnosis was made, on January 12, 1967, at the age of 73. Three specialists were immediately dispatched to the deceased: Robert Prehoda, a cryobiology researcher, Dante Brunol, a physician and biophysicist, and Robert Nelson, President of the Cryonics Society of California. They immediately injected a chemical solution into James' body to preserve his organs and tissues, then he was frozen with liquid nitrogen. He was relocated for freezing several times and placed in the facilities of the Alcor Life Extension Foundation in 1982. Today, considering the preservation and freezing technique used in 1967, specialists believe that James' brain has likely been altered, especially because vitrification was not yet possible at the time. Advocates for cryopreservation now celebrate "Bedford Day" on January 12, knowing that his body has been frozen for over half a century.

Footballer **Jean-Pierre Adams** was already well-known in his youth as a talented defender for the French national team and former player for OGC Nice and Paris Saint-Germain Football Club. Jean-Pierre Adams was born on March 10, 1948, in Dakar, Senegal. At the age of 19, he was already participating in sports competitions in the French Amateur Championship, and later he embarked on an international career with the French national team, forming the famous "black guard" with Marius Tresor. Unfortunately, he was hospitalized in March 1982 at the Edouard Herriot Hospital in Lyon for a routine operation following a ligament rupture in his knee. Things took a catastrophic turn. There was a strike by healthcare workers at this hospital, and the anesthesia was poorly administered by an anesthetist who had to attend to eight patients at once and made a dosage error. This led to a cardiac arrest, and Jean-Pierre Adams' brain was deprived of oxygen for too long, plunging him into a coma. This coma lasted for 39 years, and Jean-Pierre Adams never woke up. He passed away on September 6, 2021, at the age of 73, holding the sad record for the longest coma. He was honored during the World Cup, shifting the spotlight from his unfortunate situation, with Jean-Pierre Adams now more known for the unusually long duration of his coma than for his remarkable football achievements.

Let's also mention the case of **Cornelia Ras**, who survived a Covid-19 infection contracted on the day after her 107th birthday, during a mass attended by forty other people. Among this group, twelve people died from the virus in the following weeks. She is currently the oldest survivor of this scary virus.

WAY NUMBER SIXTEEN

WAY NUMBER SIXTEEN : BECOMING A WAR CHIEF

Not everyone becomes a general at the age of 24, like Napoleon Bonaparte. Some reveal themselves as great war leaders much later in life, gaining fame in the process. Such is the case of **Paul von Hindenburg,** born into a Prussian aristocratic family in October 1847, in Poznań on the banks of the Warta River in western Poland. His father was a Prussian officer who acquired a noble title through government positions. His mother was the daughter of a physician. At the age of 19, Hindenburg enlisted in the Prussian army and participated in the conflict with the Austrian Empire in 1866, and later in the 1870 war against the French, which earned him the rank of lieutenant general. In 1911, Hindenburg retired from military service at the age of 64. But fate had other plans and decided not to let him enjoy his peaceful and anonymous retired life for long. On June 28, 1914, a young Serbian nationalist assassinated Archduke Franz Ferdinand of Austria in Sarajevo. Through a kind of "butterfly effect," this assassination exacerbated tensions between the Triple Alliance consisting of Germany, Austria-Hungary, and Italy, and the Triple Entente comprising France, Great Britain, and Russia. In early August 1914, Germany declared war on Russia and France. Shortly after, the German Second Reich violated Belgian sovereignty, which de facto led to Britain's entry into the war, escalating the conflict into a world war. In this chain of events where the absurd leads to tragedy, Paul von Hindenburg was called back into active service to command the German Eighth Army. Quickly promoted to the rank of marshal, he distinguished himself with an initial series of victories against the Russians on the Eastern Front, propelling him to national hero status within the German Empire. Hindenburg, alongside General Erich Ludendorff, won the Battle of Tannenberg in Poland against the Russian Second Army and became a symbol of national unity and victory in Germany. Hindenburg was appointed Chief of the General Staff by the Kaiser, but Germany's defeat in 1918, which cost nearly a million lives, led to his retirement for the second time at the age of 71. In 1925, Hindenburg returned to the limelight, still revered for his victory. At Tannenberg, he was democratically elected President of the Weimar Republic. Re-elected in 1932, he held this position until 1933. The Weimar Republic did not survive the economic and social difficulties that plagued the country, and Paul von Hindenburg, despite his strong reservations about the character, was forced to appoint Adolf Hitler as Chancellor in January 1933, after the Nazi Party won the Reichstag elections in 1932. History records that after the Reichstag fire in 1933, Hindenburg offered little resistance to Hitler's consolidation of power until his death in August 1934. Hindenburg's name also remains in posterity due to the largest commercial airship ever built, bearing his name. Constructed by Zeppelin and ominously nicknamed "the Titanic of the Skies" it caught fire upon arrival in the United States, in New Jersey, in 1937. The images captured by the present press will be etched in everyone's memory, creating the symbol of one of the most spectacular air disasters and marking the end of commercial exploitation of airships. From then on, the Hindenburg disaster would be the term used to evoke this tragedy that killed a third of the hundred passengers and crew members of the airship.

Apache Chief **Cochise** was probably born around 1810 in Arizona. At that time, life expectancy was below 40 years, closer to 35 years. As a member of the Chiricahua Apache tribe, Cochise roamed the lands of his ancestors located in Arizona, New Mexico, and northern Mexico, in the Sonora region. These lands were the natural territory of the Apaches until the arrival of the first European settlers, especially the Spanish, who, coming from Mexico, began to dispute them. From initial tensions, fueled by cultural differences, to military operations conducted by the Mexican government, the scenario leading to war was triggered, based on the Apaches' fear of seeing their land increasingly encroached upon by Mexican or American settlers. In October 1860, a band of Apaches attacked the ranch of an American of Irish descent, John Ward, and kidnapped his adopted son, Felix. In 1861, Cochise was accused of planning and carrying out this abduction, and Ward sought the help of the American army to retrieve his son and bring Cochise to justice. Cochise was unexpectedly arrested and held until Felix's release. However, he managed to escape, and this event triggered a lasting conflict with the American authorities. Subsequently, Cochise and his men, fearing increasing encroachment by American settlers on their ancestral lands, conducted relentless raids on Confederate soldiers, taking refuge each time in the Dragoon Mountains, a mountain range located in southeastern Arizona. Clashes also occurred with Mexican soldiers on the other side of the border. The inhabitants of these regions demanded more protection from Mexican and American authorities, especially since these skirmishes caused hundreds of deaths, inflicted hundreds of thousands of dollars in damages, and lod many settlers to flee the area. In 1862, Cochise and 200 warriors attacked a Union military convoy threatening Confederate troops at the dawn of the Civil War. The convoy made the mistake of entering Apache Pass near Fort Bowie, and Cochise seized the opportunity to strike a major blow, which would be remembered as the Battle of Apache Pass, one of the most famous battles of the wars fought by the Chiricahua Apaches, wars that lasted a total of 24 years. Cochise and his men emerged defeated from this confrontation because the Union soldiers used an artillery piece, a weapon not possessed by the Indians. In 1872, the US government made a peace offer to Cochise to end the state of war, when Cochise was in his sixties. Cochise accepted the offer, which involved ceasing hostilities in exchange for the granting of a large reservation in southeastern Arizona for the benefit of the Apaches. Cochise died two years later, at the age of sixty four, probably from stomach cancer. His image would be further burnished ten years later when Felix resurfaced and indicated that Cochise was not among the group of Apaches who had abducted him and was not involved in the affair. Cochise had wished to be buried in an anonymous grave, and no one knows where, probably in a crevasse in Stronghold Canyon or its immediate vicinity.

Henri-Philippe Benoni Omer Joseph Pétain was born in Cauchy-à-la-Tour, in northern France, on April 24, 1856, into a family of farmers. His mother died when he was only 18 months old. At the age of 20, he joined the French army after attending the Saint-Cyr Military Academy. Over the next twenty years, until the end of the 19th century, through successive garrisons and various functions both in staff headquarters and in regiments, he rose in rank in the infantry battalions of the army. He went from the rank of captain in 1890 to major in 1900, then to colonel in 1910 after attending the Higher War School. Almost never during this journey was Pétain assigned to Indochina or African colonies, except during the Rif campaign in Morocco. At the dawn of the First World War, in 1911, and already at the age of 55, he commanded the 33rd Infantry Regiment in Arras as a colonel. Among his ranks was a young lieutenant named Charles de Gaulle. In the spring of 1914, he bought a villa, anticipating his retirement because he was convinced he would never become a general. The beginning of the conflict would quickly refute this belief. At the age of 58, he participated with his brigade in the Battle of Guise in August 1914, and then was promoted to brigadier general to replace his superior who had committed suicide. He was then given command of the 6th Division, which engaged in the Battle of the Marne. He further rose in rank a few months later by taking command of the XXIII Corps, which he led in the offensive in Artois in 1915, and then commanded the Second Army in the Champagne offensive. But it was in February 1916, when Pétain was in his sixties, that his fame as a war leader soared to the status of national hero by breaking through the German lines during the Battle of Verdun thanks to the organization of a continuous supply chain along the "Sacred Way" to the front lines.

Towards the Germans, Pétain used phrases that struck a chord: *"We will get them," "They shall not pass."* He was replaced by Nivelle, whose failed offensive at Chemin des Dames led to mutinies within the French troops. Pétain, then Commander-in-Chief, intervened to quell these mutinies and restore discipline among the demoralized armies, disillusioned by Nivelle's suicidal attacks. Pétain was made Grand Cross of the Legion of Honor in 1917 and Marshal of France in November 1918 at the time of the armistice. He was in his early sixties when he received these honors. At 62 years old, one might think that his military and civilian career is over. As everyone knows, this is not the case, and once again, it is on the occasion of a new world conflict that Philippe Pétain will be called upon. Following the French rout in May-June 1940, Paul Reynaud, the Prime Minister, brings Pétain into his cabinet as Minister of State. Pétain advocates for an armistice with Adolf Hitler, contrary to Paul Reynaud, who calls for resistance and resigns on June 16, 1940. The armistice is signed in Compiègne on June 22, 1940. It is ratified by both assemblies convened in Congress in July, which entrusts full constituent powers to Pétain. This marks the beginning of dishonor for Pétain, who at 84, takes over the government at the proposal of President Albert Lebrun and meets Hitler at Montoire on October 24, 1940.

The Third Republic no longer exists and is replaced by the "National Revolution" around the values of Work, Family, and Country, which substitute for those of Liberty, Equality, and Fraternity. The worst is yet to come: in 1941, Pétain engages France in a policy of active collaboration with Nazi Germany, and he signs the anti-Semitic ordinances regarding the status of Jews, which were negotiated by Pierre Laval with the German SS Reinhard Heydrich. This sinister policy will lead, notably, to the "Vel'dHiv roundup" in which more than 13,000 Jews, including a majority of women and children, will be arrested and deported. Pétain's end is not glorious. After the Normandy landings, he is exiled by the Germans to Sigmaringen to maintain the illusion of a still-active government. In 1945, after the victory of the Allied armies, he is sentenced to death, national indignity, and confiscation of his assets for high treason. General De Gaulle, as Head of the Provisional Government, commutes the death sentence to life imprisonment, considering Pétain's advanced age. He is stripped of all his civil and military honors. He is then deported to the island of Yeu on the Atlantic coast. Subsequently, Pétain's health deteriorates significantly, particularly his mental and cognitive faculties. His sentence is commuted to confinement in a hospital establishment. He passed away in July 1951 on the island of Yeu at the age of 95. In 1973, extremists steal his remains to demand from President Pompidou that they be transferred to the cemetery of Douaumont. Upon finding the thieves and Pétain's remains, he is reburied on the island of Yeu. Ultimately, Pétain will have known fame for the better at 60 and fame for the worse in his eighties, and that is the fame for the worst, which remains in our collective memories until today.

WAY NUMBER SEVENTEEN

WAY NUMBER SEVENTEEN : TO PHILOSOPHIZE, TO EN-GAGE IN SOCIOLOGY OR PSYCHOANALYSIS

Arthur Schopenhauer was born in February 1788 in Gdańsk, the former city of the Hanseatic League, in present-day Poland. His mother Johanna was 19 years old when his father Henri Floris was 38. The family was rather affluent, as Henri Floris was a wealthy merchant and ship owner. For him, the future of his son was already decided, and he was destined to take over his father's business. Even the choice of the name Arthur resulted from a calculation, as it was spelled similarly in various European languages, which would facilitate his son's international integration according to Henri Floris's thoughts. The annexation of Danzig by the Prussians led the family to migrate to Hamburg, then a free city of the Hanseatic League.

As a child and adolescent, Arthur discovered several European countries, including France and England, which allowed him to learn their languages. He particularly enjoyed his time in

France.His father died when he was 17, probably by suicide, and Arthur continued for a while to learn banking and commerce, in respect of his father's legacy. However, he quickly left Hamburg with his mother to go to Weimar, where she had become friends with Goethe.

Johanna Schopenhauer held salons in Weimar and wrote essays and short stories, as well as publishing biographies, including one of the Flemish painter Jan van Eyck.

Arthur encountered philosophy at the University of Göttingen, where he studied Plato and Kant. He also studied in Berlin and took an interest in literature, poetry, history, and astronomy.

He also studied the writings of Fichte, Hegel, and Schelling, and obtained a doctorate in philosophy in 1813 at the age of 25. Having moved to Dresden, he elaborated his ideas in On the Fourfold Root of the Principle of Sufficient Reason, based on the conviction that everything has a reason or cause. This major essay received very little attention except notably from Goethe, who regularly invited Schopenhauer for philosophical discussions.

Schopenhauer also developed a relationship with the philosopher Karl Christian Friedrich Krause, a former student of Fichte in Berlin.

In 1818, Arthur published The World as Will and Representation and gave lectures at the University of Berlin, which Hegel had recently joined to take over the chair of philosophy.

Schopenhauer's lectures, overshadowed by Hegel's, attracted few attendees and remained relatively obscure.

The years that followed proved difficult for Arthur Schopenhauer. Not only did his lectures fail to attract students, but he also lost a lawsuit against a seamstress roommate with whom he had a heated confrontation in a fit of anger.

His bookstore publications were also unsuccessful, and his courses at the University of Berlin attracted no one, unlike Hegel's, which were full of students.

In 1831, embittered by so much injustice, he retired to Frankfurt to live a hermit's life. He was already 43 years old.

It was only with the publication twenty years later, when he was 63 years old, in 1851, of his collection of philosophical reflections Parerga and Paralipomena that Arthur Schopenhauer began to receive some recognition. The collection was praised for its freedom of tone and originality and brought him belated success.

His work The Art of Being Right illustrates his sense of humor, and the growing influence of Schopenhauer's work would be felt on many artists, writers, or philosophers, including Nietzsche, Freud, and Bergson.

One of Schopenhauer's quotes is worth remembering: *"Talent hits a target no one else can hit; Genius hits a target no one else can see."* Arthur Schopenhauer died of a heart attack in 1860 in Frankfurt at the age of 72 and became, beyond his death, an important figure in 19th-century German philosophy.

Edgar Morin, born Edgar Nahoum, was born on July 8, 1921, in Paris. His birth was only a challenge, as his mother, suffering from heart disease, wished to abort and had used abortifacient products. Then the umbilical cord wrapped around his neck, and he emerged strangled from his mother's womb. The midwife revived him. Later, after his mother's death when he was only ten years old, a severe fever almost took his life.

During the Spanish Civil War in 1936, he joined as an anti-fascist militant in an organization that sent aid packages to Republican Spain.

Naturally, following this initial commitment, he became a member of the Communist Party in 1941 and then joined the resistance in 1942, within a communist obedience, the United Forces of Patriotic Youth. A year later, he commanded a unit of the French Forces of the Interior, an organization that merged with the National Movement of Prisoners of War and Deportees, of which François Mitterrand, who became later Président of the French Republic, was the leader.

It was during this time that he definitively adopted the pseudonym Morin, following a misinterpretation by a fellow resistance member of his first resistance name.

Self-taught, he earned degrees in law and geography, joined the CNRS (French National Center for Scientific Research) in 1950, and founded the journal Arguments in 1956. In 1959, he distanced himself further from the Communist Party, after being expelled in 1951, by publishing the book Autocritique, which expressed his disappointment with the ideology.

At the CNRS, where he became a research director, he was part of the Center for Sociological Studies directed by Georges Friedmann.

Despite his left-wing commitment and his proximity to Jean-Paul Sartre or Marguerite Duras, he did not sign the Manifesto of the 121, which declared the right to conscientious objection in the Algerian War.

In 1960, he founded the French Journal of Sociology and the journal Communications.

In the late 1960s, a rumor circulated in the city of Orléans that young women were being abducted in the dressing rooms of six clothing stores on Rue de Bourgogne, in the city center, all owned by Jewish merchants.

The purpose, according to the rumor, was to prostitute the young women abroad as part of an organized operation of trafficking white women.

This rumor, which quickly spread throughout France, was the subject of a sociological study conducted by Edgar Morin and other colleagues, given its interest and scope. This study was a success in terms of audience.

After various trips to Latin America, Edgar Morin had the opportunity to meet Jacques Monod, the author of a remarkable and noted work titled Chance and Necessity, published in 1970, which deals notably with advances in genetics, molecular biology, and the philosophical implications thereof.

This thesis could only appeal to Edgar Morin, who proclaimed himself a radical nonbeliever. He appreciated Buddhism because it is a religion without a God.

Edgar Morin began to receive a number of distinctions starting from the 1980s, when he had already passed the age of sixty. It was also from this decade that he began to write La Méthode, a work in six volumes that he completed in 2004, which constituted one of his major contributions and served as a kind of encyclopedia.

Edgar Morin, who became the theorist of complex thought, was awarded honorary doctorates from numerous foreign universities, particularly in Latin America.

From the 1990s onwards, still a young septuagenarian, he was distinguished several times in the National Order of the Legion of Honor, of which he was made a Grand Cross in 2021, and of the National Order of Merit (Grand Officer in 2012).

He also held various presidencies of associations or institutions, including the presidency of the European Agency for Culture of UNESCO and that of the scientific council of the Institute of Communication Sciences of the CNRS.

Edgar Morin, who has published numerous books and essays, remained a prolific author and published again in 2023, when he was 102 years old.

Among the many quotations from Edgar Morin, I highlight the following two :

"Old age is like a staircase, a staircase that one ascends, not a staircase that descends towards the grave. It is a staircase that one climbs where each step that comes has more value given the steps already taken. Experience gives more value to the next step. So it is

a quest, aging, of permanent change."
"Among other things, to live is to feel, to love, to be"

Sigmund Freud was born on May 6, 1856, in Freiberg, in what is now the Czech Republic, at the time part of the Austro-Hungarian Empire.

He is the eldest of a sibling group consisting of five sisters and two brothers.

As Henri Frédéric Ellenberger, a Canadian psychiatrist and criminologist, would write: *"Freud's life offers an example of a progressive social ascent from the lower middle class to the highest bourgeoisie."*

His father was a wool merchant. A few years after Sigmund's birth, the family settled in the Jewish quarter of Vienna in February 1860.

His secondary studies were quite brilliant, and he obtained an excellent mention in his maturity exam in 1873. He then enrolled at the Faculty of Medicine in Vienna, focusing mainly on biology and physiology under the renowned Ernst Brücke, director of the physiology laboratory at the University of Vienna. He graduated in 1881 and married Martha Bernays the following year. From this union, six children were born, including his youngest daughter Anna, who also distinguished herself as a psychoanalyst.

Freud devoted himself to patients with psychological disorders and now worked in Paris at the Salpêtrière Hospital with the French neurologist Jean-Martin Charcot, who treated certain mental illnesses, including hysteria, with hypnosis. His work involved neurons and cocaine, a drug he himself used between 1884 and 1895.

Returning to Vienna after a stint in Berlin in 1886, Freud learned from his work with Charcot that the beneficial effects of hypnosis do not last. With his colleague and friend Josef Breuer, he was convinced that the origin of most neuroses was due to traumatic experiences buried in the unconscious, and that by recalling them to consciousness to confront them, it was possible to improve the condition of patients by removing the psychological causes of their neurological disorders.

A disagreement arose between Freud and Breuer, as the latter felt that Freud placed too much importance on sexuality as the cause of neuroses. In particular, Freud highlighted links between infantile sexuality and the unconscious.

In 1900, at the age of 44, Sigmund Freud would publish what would become one of his major works, The Interpretation of Dreams. He proposed therapy through psychoanalytic treatment, with the setting being the "couch-chair," which replaced the traditional face-to-face arrangement on either side of the practitioner's desk.

Freud conceptualized psychoanalysis through these sessions, during which he stayed out of the patient's view as they lay on the couch to avoid influencing them.

The analytical cure was forged on the cathartic method that Freud had initiated with Breuer.

In 1909, while Freud was traveling in America, he published Five Lectures on Psychoanalysis, which dealt with psychoanalytic technique.

Freud had begun to take interest in the case of Ida Bauer, an 18-year-old woman presenting symptoms of hysteria. Freud would reveal this case in the study Dora: An Analysis of a Case of Hysteria , which is included in the five lectures and highlights the phenomenon of transference.

In 1910, Freud analyzed the composer Gustav Mahler in Holland.

In 1914, two Swiss psychiatrists, Carl Gustav Jung and Ludwig Binswanger, differentiated themselves from Freud's psychoanalysis and developed analytical psychology around the theme of the individual psyche, investigating the unconscious and the soul. It was the Zurich school that would amplify the audience of psychoanalytic theses, despite the war that paralyzed the spread of the psychoanalytic movement.

Despite criticisms and opposition to Freud's practices and ideas, psychoanalysis began to gain recognition from around 1920, when Freud was 64 years old. This was the year when Freud described the different aspects of the Ego, the Id, and the Superego. The first International Psychoanalytic Congress was held in Salzburg in 1924, in Freud's absence, and marked the expansion of the movement until 1939.

In 1932, Sigmund Freud published with Albert Einstein a summary of their correspondence on war and civilization in an essay entitled Warum Krieg (Why War ?)

Freud's publications were burned during the Nazi book burnings, and Freud had to exile himself with his wife and daughter Anna, leaving Austria first for Paris, then for London. He died in 1939 at the age of 83 from a carcinoma, influencing beyond his death numerous fields of the humanities, law, and politics, through his discoveries on the unconscious, dreams, libido and childhood sexuality, instincts, repression, and the Oedipus complex.

WAY NUMBER EIGHTEEN

WAY NUMBER EIGHTEEN : CREATING FASHION, DOING PHOTOGRAPHY

Who said, *« I never think about my age. Maybe that's the ticket. It's just a number... I've found that work is very healthy for me. I love what I do and I put my heart and soul into it ? »*

Referring to herself at 102 as a "geriatric starlet" and still having over a million followers on Facebook, **Iris Apfel (born Barrel)** was born in 1921 in the Queens neighborhood of New York to a Jewish family living on a farm, of which she would be the only child.

As a child, she made a habit of visiting the Greenwich Village neighborhood in Manhattan where she traveled by subway, which was inexpensive at the time. She enjoyed exploring antique shops and making her very first jewelry collections. Her grandmother let her play with many fabric scraps that came from the sewing work her other daughters did for charitable purposes, which gave Iris a taste for mixing colors and textures.

These playful activities of her youth would help her build the eclectic and exuberant style that would characterize her later on, with her oversized glasses and jewelry matched to fabrics of various rather vibrant colors.

She studied art history at New York University and took art courses at the University of Wisconsin.

She later worked as an interior designer for Elinor Johnson, an interior designer, and for the Women's Wear Daily newspaper, often portrayed as "The Bible of fashion." She also assisted illustrator and artist Robert Goodman, originally from Philadelphia.

Iris Apfel married Carl Apfel in 1948, and together they founded a textile company in 1950 called Old World Weavers which they ran until 1992.

The company specialized in reproductions of fabrics from the 17th, 18th, and 19th centuries.

Iris would confess that her design is classic but over the top. Her talent as a designer would offer her the opportunity to work for the White House and to work for nine presidents of the United States (Truman, Eisenhower, Kennedy, Johnson, Nixon, Ford, Carter, Reagan, and Clinton).

At that time, Iris Apfel earned her nicknames as the "First Lady of Fabric" and also "Our Lady of the Cloth."

Her design and interior restoration projects kept her busy for over forty years between 1950 and 1992.

Apfel and her husband became international globetrotters in search of new textiles, clothing, and unique furniture for interior decoration.

In 2005, when Iris Apfel was 84 years old, the Met's Costume Institute, part of the Metropolitan Museum of Art in New York, decided to center its exhibition on a selection of Iris Apfel's costume and jewelry collection.

This exhibition, about which the MET wrote : *"Iris Apfel is one of the most vivacious personalities in the worlds of fashion, textiles, and interior design, and over the past 40 years, she has cultivated a personal style that is both witty and exuberantly idiosyncratic,"* marked a radical turning point in Iris Apfel's rising fame.

After this exhibition, her fame extended beyond the New York fashion scene to transform her into an international fashion icon. In 2011, she worked on an undergraduate training program in the textiles and clothing sector at the University of Texas. Subsequently, she became the face of various cosmetic brands or the automotive industry.

In 2014, a documentary about Iris was produced, featuring prestigious testimonies from media outlets as esteemed as Vanity Fair and The Times.

In 2017, a documentary about her life, simply titled Iris, was nominated for the Emmy Awards.

In 2018, Iris Apfel designed a range of Barbie dolls wearing her legendary glasses and clothing style for Mattel.

A year later, she signed a contract with the New York City -based international modeling agency IMG.

At 103 years old, Iris Apfel continues to impart great life lessons and offer fascinating insights.

On the subject of age, Iris Apfel believed that to stay young, one must think young, meaning to maintain a sense of wonder, a sense of humor, and a constant curiosity. In an interview, she stated, *"Life can be gray and dull, so why not have fun with dressing up ?"*

She recommended always prioritizing one's personal feelings and not trying to please everyone, as she said, *"If you have to be all things to all people, you end up being nothing to nobody."*

She also believed it was a mistake to pretend to be younger than one is: *"There's nothing wrong with wrinkles. When you're older, trying to look years younger is foolish, and you are not fooling anyone. When you're seventy-five and you get a face-lift, nobody is going to think you are thirty."*

Iris Apfel, who passed away on March 1, 2024, at her residence in Palm Beach, Florida, was still active on Instagram the day before her death, with three million followers.

On June 13, 1894, **Jacques Henri Charles Auguste Lartigue** was born into a wealthy family living in Courbevoie, France.

He had the opportunity at a young age to engage in privileged activities such as oil painting, car racing, and learning the fundamentals of photography.

From the age of nine, he was seen handling a camera given to him by his father, which he used constantly to photograph his room, take portraits of his uncles and cousins, and capture his brother jumping into the water from a boat.

He enjoyed sports car driving, aviation, fashionable women on the seaside or in public gardens, and he captured all of this in his camera obscura over the years and even decades.

From 1915 to 1916, he studied painting at the Académie Julian and always considered himself more of a painter than a photographer, as talented as he was in the latter specialty.

From 1910 to 1920, he photographed extensively, more interested in the movement of things or beings than in adhering to strict rules of photographic technique.

He favored black and white photos and later experimented with a new color process called Autochrome, which allowed him to better reconcile his dual interests in painting and photography. During the 1930s and 1940s, having experienced financial setbacks, to increase his income, he sold paintings and took photographs of middle-class people during their leisure activities, far from the horrors of World War II.

Jacques Henri Lartigue's fame would change radically in the early 1960s when the Museum of Modern Art in New York dedicated an exhibition to him in 1963, when he was already 69 years old. It was following a trip to the United States that he was able to connect with a young curator from MOMA's photography department, which presented this opportunity to him.

The exhibition was a success because he departed from the posed and static portraits previously favored by photographers in his photographic works. He published a collection of his photos in 1970 titled Diary of a Century.

He was awarded the French Legion of Honor in 1975 after creating the official portrait of the new President of the French Republic, Valéry Giscard d'Estaing.

He continued his work as a photographer until his late 90s and passed away in 1986, leaving behind hundreds of photographs, 1,500 paintings, and thousands of journal pages.

Several tributes were paid to him, including a street named after him in the fifth arrondissement of Paris and a tram station in Île de France.

Rose Victoria Repetto was born in 1900 in Cannes. She married Edmond Petit in 1920, with whom she had two sons, including Roland Petit, a star dancer and founder of the Ballets des Champs-Élysées in 1945 and the Ballets de Paris in 1948, with Zizi Jeanmaire who would later become his wife.

As indicated by the Repetto house on its website: "In 1947, on the advice of her son Roland Petit, Rose Repetto set up a tiny dance shoe workshop at 22 rue de la Paix, just steps from the Paris National Opera."

Thanks to the quality and ergonomics of the shoes, success was immediate. Dancers from France and beyond flocked to the store, making Repetto the reference in the world of dance. In 1956, actress Brigitte Bardot walked through the doors of the boutique with an idea in mind: to find a shoe as lightweight as the ballet slippers she wore, but much more elegant and feminine.

Madame Repetto then created a unique ballet flat, using a technique directly inspired by the assembly of dance shoes, called "cousu retourné" (turned stitching). Thus, the first Repetto ballet flat was born, immediately synonymous with elegance and lightness.

The Cendrillon ballet flats, which Rose Repetto dedicated to Brigitte Bardot, and the presence of prestigious dancers such as Maurice Béjart, Rudolf Nureyev, Mikhail Baryshnikov, Cyril Atanassoff, and those from the Folies Bergère at her boutique, obviously greatly increased the brand's reputation and that of the boutique at 22 rue de la Paix.

In 1964, the Repetto logo was created by the Argentine artist with surrealist inspiration, Eleonor Fini, known as Leonor Fini.

In the 1970s, Serge Gainsbourg became an ambassador for the brand, having been seduced by the Zizi ballet flats, a model created by Rose Repetto for her daughter-in-law Zizi Jeanmaire.

Rose was then in her seventies.

In 1984, Rose Repetto passed away, and the brand began to decline, to the point that even dancers no longer visited the rue de la Paix boutique for their supplies.

In 1999, Jean Marc Gaucher, recently deceased in 2023, and former head of Reebok, had the opportunity to take over the struggling Repetto company.

Thanks to his management talent and partnerships with major fashion names such as Issey Miyake, Yohji Yamamoto, Comme des Garçons, and Karl Lagerfeld, Jean Marc Gaucher restored the brand and the company itself to its former glory. In 2011, Repetto had the industrial capacity to produce 500,000 pairs of ballet flats per year.

In 2012, he inaugurated a leather craft training school for Repetto in Dordogne, where several hundred apprentices familiarize themselves with the famous "cousu-retourné" technique initiated by Rose Repetto over half a century ago.

From 2013 onwards, Repetto launched its ranges of perfumes and fragrances.

Today, Repetto is present in France and Belgium and still proudly carries the name of its founder, to whom the brand owes its existence.

WAY NUMBER NINETEEN

WAY NUMBER NINETEEN : BECOMING AN ACTRESS, PRODUCER, FILMMAKER, COSTUMER

In December 1934, **Judith Olivia Dench** was born in Heworth, a neighborhood in the city of York in the north of Yorkshire, England. Her father was English, and her mother was Irish.

She studied at the Royal Central School of Speech and Drama, a school founded in 1906 and based in London. One of her classmates was Vanessa Redgrave.

Her artistic career began in 1957 in the theater, with the prestigious Royal Shakespeare Company. Her first role was Ophelia in Hamlet, and she quickly gained recognition as one of the most talented actresses of her generation. Subsequently, she played major roles in other Shakespearean plays, including Juliet in Romeo and Juliet and Lady Macbeth in Macbeth.

She was elevated to the rank of Dame Commander of the Order of the British Empire in 1988, at the age of 54, for her services to English theater.

Although heavily focused on theater, she also ventured into film starting in 1964 and remained primarily in supporting roles for over twenty years.

In 1987, she won the title of Best Supporting Actress at the 40th British Academy Film Awards for her role in the film A Room with a View (1985), where she starred alongside Maggie Smith, who won the same title at the 1987 Golden Globes.

In film, she naturally specialized in cinematic adaptations of William Shakespeare's plays, including Henry V in 1989, Hamlet in 1996, and especially Shakespeare in Love in 1999, for which she won the Academy Award for Best Supporting Actress.

However, it was especially from 1995, at the age of 61, until 2012, that her international fame skyrocketed, thanks to her role in the James Bond film series as the head of MI6 (Secret Intelligence Service).

She appeared alongside Pierce Brosnan in Golden Eye in 1995, Tomorrow Never Dies in 1997, and The World is Not Enough in 1999.

In 1999, she won a Tony Award for her role as Esme Allen in David Hare's play Amy's View performed on Broadway.

After the death of her husband Michael Williams in 2001 from lung cancer, Judy Dench went to Canada to film The Shipping New" directed by Lasse Hallström, a drama also starring Kevin Spacey and Cate Blanchett.

Also in 2001, at the age of 67, she starred in Iris, a biopic of Iris Murdoch, an Irish novelist and philosopher, alongside Kate Winslet and Hugh Bonneville, earning her an Oscar nomination the following year.

In 2002, another James Bond film with Die Another Day, followed by Casino Royale in 2006, Quantum of Solace in 2008, and then Skyfall in 2012, a highly successful film with its theme song, sung by Adele, winning the Academy Award for Best Original Song at the 85th Academy Awards in 2013, as well as the Golden Globe for Best Original Song.

For Judi Dench, who starred in this film with Daniel Craig, it was her seventh and final James Bond film, at the peak of her international fame. She was then 78 years old.

She continued to act thereafter, notably in Victoria & Abdul in 2017, where she played the role of Queen Victoria.

In 2014, addressing the prejudices of the film industry against older actresses, she stated in an interview with the Irish Examiner, "I'm tired of being told I'm too old to try something. I should be able to decide for myself if I can't do certain things and not have someone tell me I'm going to forget my lines or trip and fall on set."

Later, she also told The Hollywood Reporter, *«Age is just a number. It's something that's imposed upon you. It absolutely drives me crazy when people say to me, 'Are you going to retire ? Isn't it time you rested ?' »*

In 2020, she still made the cover of Vogue as the oldest person to do so.

She is now retired, due to a degenerative retinal disease that is gradually causing her to lose her vision.

Youn Yuh-Jung, born in June 1947, is a South Korean actress. When she was two years old, the Korean War broke out, leaving her with memories of a journey on a freight train that her family took to flee the fighting to the south of the country. Her father died when she was nine, leaving her mother to raise her alone.

Studying literature in Seoul in the late sixties, she had the opportunity to visit a television studio at TBC TV, which produced programs for children. A presenter of the show noticed her, gave her a reward for her presence on the airwaves, then she's invited back the following week, and two months later, she becomes one of the hosts of the show, embodying the role of Mister Bear. Her voice delivery and modernity appeal to the audience.

Subsequently, she paints the portrait of a royal concubine from the 17th century, which allows her to gain fame and be offered film roles. She declines them on the grounds that the scripts are all of the genre: "a poor girl meets a wealthy young man whose family opposes their marriage," and thus she finds these stories utterly uninteresting.

She then plays various roles in burlesque films, such as Woman of Fire and The Insect Woman, under the direction of Kim Ki Young, a director known for his interest in female psychology, particularly in sexualized horror films. She wins awards for best actress thanks to these films.

In 1974, she marries popular singer Jo Young-Nam, who is much more famous than her, and moves to Florida in the United States with him. While her husband studies theology, she adheres to Korean family traditions and becomes a stay-at-home mother caring for their two sons born in 1984.

Her husband cheats on her, and she divorces in 1987, forced to return to Korea to resume her career as an artist.

However, divorce was frowned upon in South Korea at that time, so her return was not easy, and she only succeeded thanks to her talent and unique personality. Initially, she thought she would never be able to return to her career after such a long break. *"No one knows me anymore. My fame has disappeared. I don't know what to do,"* she said at that point in her life. She even considered returning to the United States to take a cashier job in a supermarket to support her two children.

A young assistant director, who doesn't even know her past, then offers her a tiny role, which she eagerly accepts because she needs money. And with the talent she possesses, it's a second artistic birth that happens to her.

It wasn't until 2003, with the film A Good Lawyer's Wife by director Im Sang-Soo, in which she plays the adulterous wife of an alcoholic husband with whom she hasn't slept with for 15 years, that her career truly takes off again. The actress was then 56 years old.

In 2010, she stars in The Housemaid, an erotic and psychological thriller in which she plays the role of "Miss Cho."

In 2012, she appears in The Taste of Money,a film that mixes corruption, sex, and greed within a family conglomerate.

Her film career is punctuated by awards and nominations such as Best Actress or Best Supporting Actress. In 2016, the film Canola earns her another nomination at the 53rd Grand Bell Awards in South Korea.

In 2013, she appears in her first reality show, Sisters Over Flowers, on South Korean television, and in 2020, she makes her Hollywood debut at the age of 73 playing the role of a grandmother in a rural Arkansas family in the film Minari, a role that earns her new recognition from over 40 film critics.

In 2020, the 93rd Academy Awards honors her with the title of Best Supporting Actress.

In April 2021, Film at Lincoln Center, a non-profit organization based in New York, presents a retrospective of five of her major films, and in September of the same year, she is selected among the 100 most influential people in the world in Time 100, published by Time magazine.

In 2022, she joins the cast of Pachinko, an American TV series that depicts a saga of four generations of a Korean family.

Finally, in 2023, she signs with the Creative Artists Agency (CAA), a Los Angeles-based sports and talent agency recently acquired by billionaire François Henri Pinault.

In short, Youn Yuh-Jung's career is not over at 77 years old, and that's great !

On November 30, 1937, in England, Elizabeth, born Williams, and Colonel Francis Percy Scott give birth to young Ridley. The father is a military man, and the family lives in various places during World War II.

After the war, the family settles in the northeast of England, in County Durham, and **Ridley Scott** studies art and design at the West Hartlepool College of Art, earning a bachelor's degree in 1958. Two years later, he obtains his Master of Arts in graphic arts from the Royal College of Art in London.
Boy and Bicycle is the first black-and-white short film directed by Ridley Scott while he is still a student at the Royal College of Art in 1965, at the age of 28. Hired by the BBC, he becomes successively a cinematographer, production designer, and finally director, and works on successful English series, such as The Informe" and Z-Car.

It's from 1968 that Ridley Scott, leaving the BBC, began his directing career by founding his own production company with his brother Tony, who notably directed Top Gun in 1986, and three other partners, all of whom subsequently distinguished themselves like Alan Parker, director of Birdy and Midnight Express. In the 1970s, Ridley Scott directed numerous commercials for British television, and in 1977, at the age of 40, he directed The Duellists, adapted from a novel by Joseph Conrad, set during the Napoleonic era, which earned him an award for Best Debut at the Cannes Film Festival.

While this film received a mixed reception from the public, the next one, however, would be a "smash hit" as it was Alien, released in 1979. The film, initially coldly received by critics, turned into a huge box-office success, blending horror and science-fiction and won the Oscar for Best Visual Effects in 1980. It also launched the acting career of Sigourney Weaver, the film's heroine. Later becoming a cult film, other cinematic episodes followed, including Alien : Covenant directed in 2017 by Ridley. In 1982, Ridley Scott released Blade Runner, a sort of science-fiction thriller set in Los Angeles, illustrating a policeman battling androids called replicants. Initially, the film didn't perform well in the United States but was a success overseas and became a major work in the cyberpunk genre and post-apocalyptic universes.

In 1984, Ridley Scott, who had never stopped making commercials, directed the one for Apple for the Macintosh, notably for the 1984 Super Bowl. This ad, inspired by George Orwell's novel 1984, was very noticed. In 1985, Ridley Scott directed Legend, a fairy tale with Tom Cruise, which would become successful thanks to its DVD version. In the following years, Ridley Scott aimed to break out of the category he had been pigeonholed into, that of a very talented advertiser for special effects, to be more recognized as a director of films closer to everyday reality.

He notably produced Black Rain in 1989, a police film with Michael Douglas and Andy Garcia, set in Japan in the yakuza milieu. As often with Ridley Scott, the critics initially shunned the film before the public transformed it into a commercial success afterward. In 1991, Ridley made a big splash by directing Thelma & Louise, a film that depicts the escapade of two women using weapons to combat male violence, starring actresses Susan Sarandon and Geena Davis, and actor Brad Pitt, whose career this film launched. While this film achieved commercial success and won the Oscar for Best Original Screenplay, the next one, 1492: Conquest of Paradise, with Gérard Depardieu, was a resounding failure that kept Ridley Scott away from the sets for almost five years.

It was in 2000, when Ridley was now 63 years old, that he directed and signed Gladiator" one of his biggest commercial successes.

This film, set in the time of the Roman Empire, starring Russell Crowe and Richard Harris, depicts the adventures of a Roman general grappling with Emperor Commodus. The film grossed hundreds of millions of dollars and won five Oscars, including Best Picture and Best Actor for Russell Crowe. In 2001, Black Hawk Down was released, inspired by the civil war in Somalia during the 1990s, and it was a modest commercial success, despite rather good reviews upon release this time.

In addition to his talent, Ridley Scott is known for his very strong work ethic. He would prove it again later, with various more or less successful films such as A Good Year with actress Marion Cotillard, American Gangster, again with Russell Crowe in a leading role. He released Prometheus in 2012, marking his return to science-fiction and still grossing over $400 million.

After various films, including Exodus in 2014, Ridley Scott produced a huge science-fiction success in 2015 with The Martian, in which an astronaut played by Matt Damon survives alone on the red planet. The film was a hit, garnered seven Oscar nominations, including Best Picture, and grossed over $600 million at the box-office. In 2015, Ridley also married Giannina Facio, an actress and former showgirl, 18 years his junior, whom Ridley has featured in almost all of his films since 1999. The second episode of Blade Runner was released in 2018 under the title Blade Runner 2049, with Harrison Ford once again, and just after Alien Covenant.

In 2021, the film House of Gucci, starring Lady Gaga, Al Pacino, and Adam Driver, tells the story and murder, on the orders of his ex-wife Patrizia Reggiani, of Maurizio Gucci in Milan in 1995. In 2023, at 86 years old, Ridley Scott released Napoleon and returned to historical films and his interest for the Napoleonic epic. The reviews in France, the country of the Emperor, are mediocre, but the public reception of the film is rather good.

Latest news has it that at 86, Ridley Scott is preparing to shoot a biopic feature film about the Bee Gees, negotiating with Paramount Pictures, and working on a western project and the movie Gladiator 2.

Ann Roth was born in Hanover, Pennsylvania, the Quaker State, on October 30, 1931, to Eleanor and James Roth. In 1953, she earned a degree from the College of Fine Arts at Carnegie Mellon University in Pittsburgh. She began painting sets and landscapes for the Pittsburgh Opera.

There, at the Bucks County Playhouse theater in New Hope, she met Irene Sharaff, a famous costume designer who had created costumes for renowned Broadway shows and films such as West Side Story, Cleopatra, Who's Afraid of Virginia Woolf" and An American in Paris.
Irene Sharaff discouraged her from further pursuing a career as a set decorator, stating that, *"it's not a place for women."*

However, she offered Ann Roth the opportunity to join her in California to assist in making costumes for the film Brigadoon, shot in 1954 near Los Angeles but set in Scotland, starring Gene Kelly.

Irene Sharaff enlisted Ann Roth for five subsequent films and five Broadway shows. With this apprenticeship and initiation, Ann Roth would now spread her wings and design costumes for her first Hollywood film in 1964, The World of Henry Orient, starring Peter Sellers.
The rest of her career is marked by key milestones. In 1969, she notably costumed Dustin Hoffman in Midnight Cowboy, then de-

signed a short black nightgown with pink hands supporting the breasts, inspired by a porn magazine, for Barbara Streisand in The Owl and the Pussycat in 1970. She would revisit this theme in 2013 for the play The Nance written by Douglas Carter Beane. This earned Ann Roth a Tony Award for costume design.

In Klute in 1971, she dressed Jane Fonda, who played the role of a call girl. In 1984, for the film Places in the Heart, Ann Roth was nominated for an Oscar for Best Costume Design for the costumes she created for actress Sally Field. The real Oscar, for Best Costume Design, would come later, in 1997 when Ann was already 66 years old, for her work as a costume designer in The English Patient, directed by Anthony Minghella and starring actresses Kristin Scott Thomas and Juliette Binoche. To accomplish this work, Ann Roth delved into the archives of the British Royal Geographical Society in London and photos from the 1930s taken by American photographer Elizabeth Miller, a student of Man Ray.

In 2004, she adorned Natalie Portman with a $19 pink wig in the film Closer, which earned Natalie Portman the Oscar for Best Supporting Actress. In 2017, for Steven Spielberg's film The Post, she created costumes for Tom Hanks and Meryl Streep.

Throughout her career, Ann Roth collaborated with nearly all the stars of film-making : Dino De Laurentiis, Mike Nichols, Steven Spielberg, John Schlesinger, Anthony Minghella, Brian De Palma, Jack O'Brien, and many others like George Roy Hill or Stephen Daldry.
In 2020, at the age of 89, Ann Roth designed costumes for the film Ma Rainey's Black Bottom, directed by George C. Wolfe, with actress Viola Davis playing the blues singer Ma Rainey. This film earned Ann Roth the Oscar for Best Costume Design in 2021.

In June 2021, Ann Roth told journalist Anna Wyckoff in an interview titled The Person in the Mirror, *"The important thing for an actor is to know that you are there to help them find their character. You are there for them, not for yourself, to say that their clothing comes from Ann Roth."* In 2023, in Greta Gerwig's film Barbie, Ann Roth, a friend of the director, was chosen to deliver a brief but moving line at a bus stop to actress Margot Robbie, who portrays Barbie.

In an interview with The New York Times in July 2023, Anne Roth said in preamble, *"Don't call me amazing. Don't tell me I'm a legendary 91-year-old. Don't remind me that I'm the oldest person in the Barbie movie."*

WAY NUMBER TWENTY

WAY NUMBER TWENTY : STARTING A FAMILY AND HAVING CHILDREN

Ramjit Raghav was born in India in the state of Haryana, northwest of Delhi, apparently in 1916, and began earning his living as a wrestler before becoming a farmer. He primarily claims to be vegetarian, mainly eating almonds, accompanied by milk and butter. For him, this diet of vegetables and grains is a guarantee of his longevity, and above all, of his virility. Ramjit also declares himself to be sober and never drinks alcohol.

His life is as regular as clockwork-: every God-given day, he wakes up at 5 am., works in the fields in the morning, takes a nap from one to two hours in the afternoon, and goes to bed at 8 pm.

Ramjit Raghav first appeared in the spotlight in 2010, at the supposed age of 94, claiming to be the world's oldest father when his 49-year-old wife gave birth to a boy, whom the couple named Bikramjeet. Two years later, the couple welcomed a second son named Ranjeet. Later, they decided against having a third child together, not because of Ramjit's advanced age but only for financial reasons. Ramjit's $9.50 pension from the government of his state proves to be insufficient to cover the expenses of a large family.

In November 2012, the American organization PETA (People for the Ethical Treatment of Animals) chose Ramjit Raghav to be its international ambassador on the grounds that only vegetarians can still stay healthy at 96 years old. In 2013, his wife Shakuntala Devi suddenly left him, the day before Ranjeet's first birthday, taking their son with her. Ramjit declared himself devastated by this news, leaving him alone at 97 within the four walls of his home.

Ramjit told the Mirror newspaper that accustomed to making love three to four times a night with Devi, he had to moderate his sex life since becoming a father and for the sake of his children. Ramjit, who had remained single before, had met Devi in a Muslim mausoleum ten years earlier, on a rainy day, and they had fallen in love while doing yoga together.

Ramjit Raghav died in 2020 in a house fire at the age of 104.

Omkari Panwar gave birth to twins, a boy and a girl, by cesarean section at 34 weeks of gestation. Up until then, nothing extraordinary, but she has just turned 70, while her husband is seventy-seven.

The Panwar couple, already parents of two daughters and grandparents to five grandchildren, absolutely wished to have a male heir, capable of benefiting from a dowry upon his marriage, and also to work their land.

To achieve their goal, the Panwar couple resort to in vitro fertilization, and to finance the process which is well beyond their means, they sell their livestock, mortgage their land, sacrifice their meager savings, and use the credit allowed by their credit card.

Omkari's pregnancy is not a smooth journey-: it is painful and chaotic, but Omkari has seen worse and she admits that sometimes one must suffer to obtain the good one desires. Furthermore, she and her husband pray to God, his Saints every day, and they often visit religious places to seek help from Heaven in this trial.

Omkari gives birth prematurely at Muzaffarnagar hospital, seven hours' drive north of New Delhi, but everything goes well and Omkari's husband declares himself very happy and proud to be a father again.

Omkari is recognized as the world's oldest mother and has been mentioned by the international press in this regard.

Some already well-known personalities have also made headlines, not for a new film, a new single, a new book, or a new play, but through late fatherhood.

For instance, **Robert De Niro** had the pleasure in April 2023, at the age of 80, of being the proud father of a little Gia Virginia Chen De Niro, the result of his union with Tiffany Chen, 45 years old.

For Robert De Niro, this was his seventh child, which he had, in the end, from four different women.

Shortly after childbirth, Tiffany Chen suffered from Bell's palsy, a temporary paralysis of the face that can be a complication following pregnancy.

Following in the footsteps of Robert De Niro, **Al Pacino,** the legendary actor from *The Godfather* or *Scarface,* was delighted in 2023, at the age of 83, to welcome into his home his newborn son Roman, with his partner Noor Alfallah, 29 years old. For him, Roman is his fourth child, conceived with three different women, two twins from actress Beverly D'Angelo, and a daughter, Julie Marie, from his former coach Jan Tarrant.

Since we're on the topic, let's also acknowledge **Anthony Quinn** in this book, the unforgettable character from *Zorba the Greek* and multiple Academy Award winner, who had two children with his secretary Katherine Benvin, whom he met when he was 70 and she was 23.

Anthony Quinn then becomes the proud father of Antonia Patricia Rose and Ryan Nicholas, when he is respectively 78 and 81 years old. Katherine Benvin reportedly said, *"I thought that in your sixties, people just sit in a chair and more or less wait to die."*

Then I met Quinn in a tracksuit after a jog, who told me, *"My life is a mess. I'm painting something, I'm going to do a play, I'm making a movie, and I'm also writing a screenplay. I need someone to help me."*

WAY TWENTY ONE

WAY NUMBER TWENTY-ONE : SEDUCE AND COURT

In the early 1620's, possibly in 1623 according to her account or rather on November 10, 1620 according to other sources, Anne was born in Paris, daughter of Henri de Lenclos and Marie-Barbe de la Marche, quickly nicknamed Ninon.

Under the guidance of her father, an openly libertine, cultured, and skilled lute player, young **Ninon de Lenclos** not only learned to play the lute but also delved into literature.

She read Montaigne's Essays, which fascinated her, as well as other great classics, allowing her to impress in the various salons where her devout mother introduced her. Ninon soon enriched her conversation by practicing the harpsichord, which she learned after the lute.

She was curious about everything, learned Spanish and Italian, as well as sciences, and became a woman of letters. She felt libertine like her father and defended Epicureanism, a philosophy centered on achieving happiness through the satisfaction of one's natural and necessary desires.

In 1632, her father became involved in a sordid affair of adultery followed by a murder. He fled the marital home.

Ninon was 16 years old and took her first lover, the first of many on a long list ! She now lives, at her mother's initiative, in the Marais district of Paris, near the Place Royale, where the high aristocracy resides and has its habits, especially of libertinage.

The first lover quickly disappears, but Ninon, who has gained experience in the field of seduction, is quickly supported by a counselor of the Parliament.

In 1642, her mother dies, and the « Precieuses » who animate the salons of the Marais start to ignore Ninon, whose respectability is still to be built.

She then comes under the benevolent wing of Marion Delorme, a courtesan at the peak of her fame and former mistress of Richelieu and Monsieur de Cinq Mars.

Also residing at Place Royale, the duo Ninon de Lenclos and Marion Delorme frequent the entire gallant Paris of young court lords. Marion is prettier than Ninon but less witty, and she dies at 36 of antimony poisoning.

Ninon chooses and collects lovers : Le Grand Condé, cousin of Louis XIV, François de la Rochefoucauld, Marshal d'Estrées, the astronomer Christian Huyghens. She classifies her lovers into three categories, depending on whether they pay her, sigh without hope, or are her whims or current crush.

Louis de Mornay, Marquis of Villarceaux and captain of the king's hunt, belongs to this last category and will give a son to Ninon. As Villarceaux is married, this will result in Ninon being briefly confined in a convent by order of Queen Anne of Austria.

Even though Manon trades in gallantry, to the point that she is nicknamed "Our Lady of Loves," by frequenting the most influential men of the kingdom with a fierce appetite, she also seduces with her culture, wit, and intelligence.

Her activity as a courtesan has enriched her and granted her true financial independence. Therefore, upon leaving the convent, she becomes more discreet about her sexual commerce, which she nevertheless continues until the age of 77, and turns more towards hosting her salon, which she opens in 1667 at the Hôtel de Sagonne, approaching her fifties.

She receives Molière, whom she feels close to, and advises him on Tartuffe, and soon the most famous people in culture gather at her place: La Rochefoucauld, a former lover, Scarron, Fontenelle, Françoise d'Aubigné, Jean-Baptiste Lully, Jean de la Fontaine, Nicolas Boileau, the Princess Palatine, the Duke of Saint-Simon, Charles Perrault, Jean Racine, and Philippe d'Orléans.

The spirit of her salon is libertine and atheistic. Henri de Sévigné, husband of the Marquise, is a pillar of her salon where everyone shares their philosophical reflections.

For over thirty years, Ninon de Lenclos acquired real renown through her extensive correspondence with the Marquis de Sévigné, which developed her philosophical vision of love, Epicureanism, ethics, metaphysics, and naturalism.

For her, love and its passions always dominate humans in their moral choices. Love and sexuality bring the greatest pleasures of life and lift us out of routine. In 1659, she was credited with writing a pamphlet defending living independently of any religious influence.

Voltaire, whom she knew when he was a young boy, wrote in 1751, as a tribute to her, "Dialogue between Madame de Maintenon and Mademoiselle de Lenclos," in which a philosophical dialogue is established between these two great friends on old age. Ninon died on October 17, 1705, in the late afternoon at the age of 85.

Massimo Gargia was born in Naples, Italy, on August 20, 1940, to an engineer father and a homemaker mother. Very soon he grew tired of Neapolitan life and began to discover another life in Capri, where he encountered the jet-set and found success with women. He would later discover the cruelty of the jet set by noticing how quickly it rejects those who suddenly have no success or money, like a cherry pit.

He then decided to study in Rome, supposedly at the Ministry of Foreign Affairs, but it was just an excuse given to his parents to leave. At 22, he moved to Paris and seduced for the first time a very wealthy woman, one of the daughters of the Agnelli dynasty. He obtained a law degree from the University of Naples, in order to still be able to pursue a career in the Ministry of Foreign Affairs. One of his mistresses who would become a lifelong friend is Françoise Sagan. She was very generous with Massimo and gave him sumptuous gifts.

He had a brief affair with Greta Garbo and became friends with Gina Lollobrigida.

At 40, as he aged, Massimo realized that if he wanted to continue mingling with the jet set, he could no longer rely solely on his success with wealthy women. He needed to find something else and turned to public relations and organizing parties for the wealthy.

It was in 1978 precisely that he founded and directed the magazine The Best with the Italian playboy Giorgio Pavone. They came up with the idea of rewarding personalities every year. In the world of fashion and elegance, they awarded a trophy from their magazine The Best.

In 1985, he obtained small roles in a few films, including Milady with Arielle Dombasle. Massimo openly identifies as bisexual and married Francine Crescent, former editor-in-chief of Vogue France, in 1991. Celebrities such as Rihanna or Madonna are paid a hefty sum to attend events, with their fees sometimes exceeding one million euros for one night of presence.

As Massimo indicated in August 2023 in an interview with Jordan De Luxe, his participation in the 2004 television show La Ferme des Célébrités changed his life by greatly expanding his fame beyond just the jet set and into popular circles. He was 64 years old at the time.

After this show, Massimo started getting paid to attend events himself, which allowed him to finance the medical care of his wife, who was suffering from a rare form of Parkinson's disease and passed away in 2008.

Also in 2004, Massimo recorded a single, a jet-set parody of a hit by the group O-Zone, titled "Ma Ce Ki ? " This single made it into the best-selling list of the year 2004.

In 2008, Massimo was a member of the jury for Mister France, and in 2009, he chaired the jury of the Top Model Belgium show, hosted by Adriana Karambeu and Jérémy Urbain.

Throughout the 2000s, Massimo Gargia also emerged as an author and published numerous books, including Jet-Set: Memoirs of a Playboy"in 2000, The Journal of Massimo: A Year in the Life of a Jet-Setter in 2004, The Millionaire's Guide in 2007, The Woman of My Life in 2008, and The Double Life in 2018.

Massimo, who was 84 years old in August 2024, accepts aging only because he manages to maintain more or less the same lifestyle as when he was younger. Despite being devoid of fortune in his advanced retirement age, he continues to organize parties for his billionaire friends, especially in Switzerland, in Gstaad, or on the French Riviera, in Cannes and Saint-Tropez.

Sári Gábor was born in February 1917 in Budapest, Hungary. When fame seized her, it would be under the name **Zsa Zsa Gabor.**

At 13, she studied in Switzerland and caught the attention of the opera singer Richard Tauber, who introduced her somewhat to the world of entertainment.

After some performances in theater and operetta in Vienna, her first notable achievement was being elected Miss Hungary in 1936.

When one considers the richness of Zsa Zsa Gabor's romantic journey, the year 1937 marks the beginning as she finds her first husband, an official from the Turkish government who was 35 years old.

Four years later, the two spouses agreed to a divorce, while Zsa Zsa and her mother settled in the United States to escape Nazism, as the family was Jewish.

The young woman wasted no time, quickly becoming acquainted with Conrad Nicholson Hilton, the founder of the hotel chain of the same name, in a club. The flirtation quickly turned into an official union that resulted in the birth of a daughter, Francesca. However, this did not last long, as the couple divorced in 1947.

Her third marriage was in 1949 to the actor George Sanders, who would later remarry Magda, one of Zsa Zsa's two sisters.

In 1952, Zsa Zsa played a role in John Huston's film Moulin Rouge, and later in Lili. From these years and over the next forty, she appeared frequently on television in various shows, talk-shows, game shows, or comedies. In the 1960s, she played the criminal Minerva in the series Batman. She also starred in films in Hollywood, notably with Orson Welles in Touch of Evil, or in Europe, and in 1958 she won the Golden Globe for the most glamorous actress.

Her way of pronouncing "darling" as "dah-link" charmed and gave her a distinctive style.

Zsa Zsa went through a series of marriages and divorces. These included the financier Herbert Hutner, the oil magnate Joshua

Cosden, the inventor Jack Ryan, the lawyer Michael O'Hara, and the actor Felipe de Alba.

Her last marriage, to Prince Frederick von Anhalt, who was 30 years her junior and celebrated in 1986, would be much more enduring, lasting until her death in 2016. In total, she had nine marriages.

Beyond these official unions, Zsa Zsa did not hide having had numerous other affairs with various celebrities, such as Atatürk, Sean Connery, Frank Sinatra, Richard Burton, and having rejected advances from others such as John F. Kennedy, Elvis Presley, or Henry Fonda.

This tumultuous and spectacular love life contributed as much to Zsa Zsa's fame as her film career. Her image as a femme fatale or courtesan is now firmly established.

She declares, *"I am a good housekeeper. Every time I divorce, I keep the house,"* and also, *"I have never hated a man enough to give him back his diamonds."*

In 2009, Zsa Zsa returned to the headlines of the tabloids when her lawyer revealed that she was one of the victims of the Bernard Madoff scandal and had lost millions of dollars in this fraud.

Even in her 70s, she was seen until the mid-1990s, performing in theater, appearing in TV series, or having roles in movies. Her last appearance was in the film A Very Brady Sequel in 1996, when she was 79 years old.

Zsa Zsa's health has always been a problem. When she was young, she suffered from depression and bipolar disorder.

Starting in 2002, when she was 85 years old, troubles accumulated. After a partial paralysis following a car crash, she had a stroke in 2005, then a fall in 2010, followed by an amputation of her right leg in 2011 to ward off an infection.

She passed away in Los Angeles from a heart attack in December 2016, just shy of her one hundredth birthday.

WAY NUMBER TWENTY TWO

WAY NUMBER TWENTY TWO : LOVING SEX

Richard Lemieuvre was born in Marseille on August 12, 1942. While this name would remain completely unknown until this day, his pseudonym **Richard Allan** is, however, in the memories of all those who watched the dozens of pornographic films he made in the 1970s-1980s.

It's impossible to name all the titles in this book at once out of discretion, but also because their list is long, which indeed reflects Richard Allan's exceptional qualities as a performer.

Let's still mention the film Queue de Béton (Concrete Dick) in 1978, which earned him his reputation for the rest of his porn actor career, or Les bas de soie noire (Black Silk Stockings) in 1981, which remains a classic of the French Golden Age of X.

Of course, most of the other titles are very explicit, with the following giving a glimpse : French érection in 1976, Le feu à la minette (Pussy in Fire) and Sophie aime les sucettes (Sophie likes lollipops) in 1978, La cage aux partouzes (The Orgy Cage) in 1977,

La grande lèche (The Big Lick) in 1979, L'aubergine est bien farcie (The Eggplant is well stuffed) in 1981, Les Tontons tringleurs (The Uncles Whore) in 1999.

Since the sixties, when he was in his twenties, his strong interest in sex led him to participate in orgies, even as during the day, he works in construction and import-export.

Married to Liliane, the couple quickly becomes regulars at swingers' clubs to indulge in the group sex they enjoy.

Later, he would describe the world of Parisian nightlife that he frequented diligently, where celebrities and perfect strangers mingle freely in organized orgies.

An attempt at a pornographic photo novel is aborted because Richard Allan is a little too stressed by the camera and can't get aroused.

Nevertheless, he applies himself to dissociate his mind from his virile organ, and as a result, he no longer experiences performance anxiety. He now embarks on shooting pornographic films with the French female stars of the industry : Claudine Beccarie, Sylvia Bourdon, Brigitte Lahaie, Marilyn Jess, Karine Gambier.

Richard Allan will shoot more than 400 porn films until 1984, the year he turns 42 and retires, without any pun intended. At the same time, he plays minor roles in non-pornographic films, such as La guerre des polices (The Police War) by Robin Davis in 1979 and Police in 1985 by Maurice Pialat.

However, he returns to the scene in 1999, at the age of 57, in Les Tontons Tringleurs, where he reunites with his comrade Alban Ceray, as well as porn actors Dominique Aveline and Roberto Malone, all in their fifties, sometimes well beyond. The actresses in the film, on the other hand, are much younger than these soon-to-be porn grandpas.

In 2007, a French screenwriter and director made the film Brigitte and me, starring female porn star Brigitte Lahaie and Richard Allan. Against the backdrop of a love story between these two actors, it evokes, based on archives, the golden age of X cinema and the sexual liberation of women in the 1970s-1980s. In 2010, Richard Allan published his memoirs under the title 8000 Women, supposedly representing the number of women he had copulated with, a title imposed by his publisher, as it was not his choice.

Following the bankruptcy of the publisher, Richard Allan reissued his book in 2018 under the title Démon de Vénus.
In 2022, Richard, now 80 years old, still going strong, so to speak, publishes the book Aventures Sextraordinaires, a 352-page book prefaced by Brigitte Lahaie. Enriched with hundreds of photos and anecdotes, it looks back on Richard Allan's acting career and the "enchanted parenthesis" that porn was for him.

In the realm of sex, the case of **Shigeo Tokuda** is even more astonishing. Born in Tokyo on August 18, 1934, Shigeo Tokuda worked as a tour guide until his retirement at the age of 60. Throughout his life up to that point, nothing extraordinary or surprising had happened to Shigeo that could have brought him into the spotlight, even for a day.
In retirement, Tokuda became bored and started watching porn to pass the time. He eventually got to know a porn film director and became friends with him. The director shared an observation with him : there was an audience eager for porn featuring elderly people and younger actresses. Tokuda was offered a leading role, which he enthusiastically accepted. However, Tokuda is no Adonis. He is short, less than 1.60 meters tall, and bald.
From then on, he found his second career in his sixties and went on to make 350 pornographic videos. Japan, with a population of approximately 124 million, is facing an increasingly critical aging population. Among them, more than 30 million people are over 65 years old.

This phenomenon greatly helped Tokuda build his porn actor career. The adult video industry in Japan partly targets this elderly audience, who identify with older actors or young actors having intercourse on camera with mature women, well into their thirties. Furthermore, this senior generation in Japan experienced a somewhat repressed youth due to the rigidity and conformity of Japanese society at that time.

Tokuda initially worked for Ruby Productions studios with actresses of various ages, and later with Glory Quest studios, which specialize more in X-rated videos involving older male actors, often over 70 years old. In this vein, in 2004, Glory Quest launched a series titled Maniac Training of Lolitas, which quickly became popular. It was followed in 2006 by another successful series titled Forbidden Elderly Care.

At the age of 70, Tokuda, who had suffered a heart attack, became, through these series, a true icon of the rapidly growing Japanese "silver porn" industry. During an interview on Canal+, Tokuda stated, *"I believe today that porn for the elderly is necessary, and I encourage as many elderly people as possible to join us."*

In 2008, an American channel aired a documentary about Tokuda, causing a sensation. On one of his latest CD-ROMs that he exhibited at the time, it was written: *"Ah, what happiness ! Do not fear aging ! Desire is the best remedy !"* Of course, he has been asked the same question several times, *"What secret explains your sexual vitality? "* His answer lies in a lifestyle excluding any medication, based on a diet of eggs and vegetables, and daily walks. He also believes that as soon as the camera rolls, his imagination takes over and that helps him. Tokuda's example inspired Japanese X producers to expand the winning formula by featuring aged porn actresses, sometimes over 70 years old, as well.

Tokuda is listed in the Guinness World Records as the oldest porn actor in the world. His family only discovered his X-rated activities when he was 74 years old, and his wife doesn't seem to have been offended, just worried about his health, fearing he might overwork himself !

In 2021, Tokuda was still involved in the X-rated industry.

Dominique Alderweireld was born in Annoeullin in the North of France on February 5, 1949. He had a difficult childhood and would later say that he could only bathe once a week during that time because his parents were poor.

At the age of 5, his parents moved to the city of Lille, into a sordid apartment on Baignerie Street, a name given to brothels in the Middle Ages.

He performed poorly in school, failed his sixth grade three times, mainly due to dyslexia. He was sent to the Jesuits, but the only result that would come out of it would be his aversion to religion and his anti-clericalism.

His first burglary at the age of 17 and his first encounter with a "marmite" (prostitute) at 18, whom he quickly became the pimp of.

He learned karate and went with his teacher to extort money from clients picked up in gay bars in the city. He met Frédérique, who seduced men to extract money from them.

Dominique ensured her safety during her paid encounters and collected the proceeds.

From there, Dominique Alderweireld, later nicknamed "Dodo la Saumure," (Dodo the brine) began to string together odd jobs and shady schemes and scams. At one point, he was seen as a real estate agent for the African leader Félix Houphouët-Boigny.

In 1970, he opened his first bar in Lille, then in Dunkirk with clandestine slot machines. He earned his nickname Dodo la Saumure, in reference to his first name Dominique and to the brine used to preserve mackerels (pimps in French) !

Taking advantage of the tolerance granted by Belgian law on prostitution, he opened "massage parlors" in Belgium and upscale bars. He even had the audacity to open a brothel in the city of Tournai, right across from the police station, even though while prostitution is legal in Belgium, pimping is illegal under the law.

In 1986, he met Marie, a woman from a good family in her forties eager to find a father for her child. Despite Dodo la Saumure's criminal past, including car thefts, counterfeit trafficking, and pimping, the couple settled down, but not for long, as Marie quickly kicked him out of their marital home.

His daughter Camille was born in October 1987 in the 14th arrondissement of Paris, while he was serving a prison sentence at Fleury-Mérogis. He named his daughter Camille, as a tribute to a Corsican gangster nicknamed that, whom he admired and who had just been murdered. Dodo would abandon his daughter after his breakup with Marie, knowing he would have two more daughters with different women.

By the end of the period from 2000 to 2009, Dodo was running at least 16 brothels in various Belgian localities, frequented notably by some French personalities who crossed the French border to enjoy paid pleasures without risk.

It was in 2011 that Dodo la Saumure would make headlines nationally and even internationally thanks, if one can say so, to the good offices of Dominique Strauss-Kahn, former Minister of Finance.

In May 2011, Dominique Strauss-Kahn (nicknamed DSK), former Minister and Managing Director of the International Monetary Fund (IMF), was arrested at John Fitzgerald Kennedy Airport in New York, on charge of rape, sexual assault, and unlawful imprisonment filed by a hotel maid at the Sofitel where he had just stayed in Manhattan.

The news was a bombshell, as it not only involved the leader of one of the world's most reputable financial institutions, but

Strauss-Kahn was also the favorite for the next presidential election in France, where polls predicted he would defeat the French Président Nicolas Sarkozy.

Among the many developments in the case, the press reveals that a certain René Kojfer, in charge of public relations for the Carlton and Les Tours hotels in Lille, organizes "parties fines" involving prostitutes and notable figures, including Dominique Strauss Kahn and the Divisional Commissioner of Police of Lille, Jean-Christophe Lagarde.

The girls are selected and provided by Dodo la Saumure, who is then living with a prostitute named Béa, who herself participated in "parties fines" (orgies) with Strauss-Kahn both in Paris and in Washington DC, the headquarters of the IMF. Judicial procedures unfold, and their coverage in all media popularizes the name and colorful personality of Dodo la Saumure, who is then 62 years old. In 2012 and 2013, he is a guest on several TV shows, including Ce soir ou jamais (Tonight or Never) and Touche pas à mon poste. (Don't touch my TV set). He also becomes the subject of a music video by rapper Seth Gueko in 2013.

Like Dominique Strauss Kahn himself, Dodo la Saumure ultimately benefits from an acquittal in this case in 2015.

In 2014, he still operates five "massage parlors," one of which he names the "DSK" for "Dodo Sex Klub." That same year, he receives a suspended sentence of five years from the Court of Appeal of Hainaut in Mons, for procuring and solicitation to debauchery.

A provocateur, Dodo la Saumure declares in opposition to the MeToo movement: *"MeToo, I don't know what it is. As for women's rights, I'm against them; I'm for the rights of humanity."*

In 2022, at 73 years old, he welcomed a new relaxation of Belgian law on procuring, which should allow him to reopen brothels, this time entirely legally.

In the category of elderly pimps, let's also mention the case of the American **Dennis Hof.** Born in 1946 in Phoenix, Arizona, he first became a gas station manager in Arizona and Nevada.

In 1992, he bought and renovated The Moonlite BunnyRanch, a brothel located 10km from Carson City, Nevada. This brothel was established in 1955 and discreetly operated its prostitution activities until 1971, when the state of Nevada gave it legal status.

Dennis Hof was initially a regular client of the establishment, but seeing the opportunity to buy it for seven hundred thousand dollars, he acquired it and refurbished all the interior decorations and facilities for five hundred thousand dollars more.

Under Hof's leadership, the business thrives and attracts various personalities, including the Governor of Minnesota, a former wrestler named Jesse Ventura.

In 2002, the ranch is the subject of a series on HBO in the documentary series America Undercover, in the form of a show titled Cathouse. This series, which runs until 2007, is a great success and contributes to boosting Hof's fame, who is now in his sixties. In 2008 and 2012, he supports the candidate Ron Paul in the presidential elections and then runs for local elections in Nevada, aligning himself with the Republican camp with varying degrees of success.

In 2009, access to the ranch is facilitated by the Nevada Department of Transportation, which constructs a road directly linking it to U.S. Highway 50, which connects California to Maryland.

Shortly thereafter, Hof buys another nearby brothel, Madame Kitty's Fantasy Ranch,and first renames it the BunnyRanch Two, then The Love Ranch in 2008.

In 2016 and 2017, Hof was accused by former employees of his ranches of raping and sexually abusing them, but he escapes prosecution.

In 2018, he is again a candidate in the primaries in Nevada, but dies two days after his 72nd birthday and so close to the election day that he is declared the winner posthumously over his Democratic opponent.

CHAPTER 26

WAY NUMBER TWENTY THREE

WAY NUMBER TWENTY-THREE : PROPHECY, DOING GOOD

On August 26, 1910, in Skopje, Macedonia, Anjezë Gonxhe Bojaxhiu was born, who would later gain worldwide fame as a nun under the name **Mother Teresa.** During her childhood, her parents called her Gonxha Agnès.

Her family is Albanian, Christian, and practices Catholicism, so the young girl receives her first communion at the age of five and a half and her confirmation the following year.

Her father, an entrepreneur and merchant, suddenly dies of a heart attack when she is nine years old, a tragic event that plunges the family into financial difficulties.

The mother, Drane, faces this difficult situation by opening a sewing workshop and manages to raise her children with love and firmness. Young Gonxha Agnès emerges strengthened in her religious vocation from this pious and dignified family atmosphere, especially as she actively engages during this time within the local Jesuit parish of the Sacred Heart

From the age of twelve, she considers dedicating herself to God, and after a pilgrimage to the Marian sanctuary of Letnica, located in the black mountain of Skopje, her vocation is fully confirmed. At eighteen, in 1928, she leaves the family home and her native land to join the Institute of the Blessed Virgin Mary, also known as the Sisters of Loreto, in Ireland, near Dublin, where she will learn English.

At the end of 1928, she travels to India, to Calcutta, to begin her novitiate there. Seeing the misery prevailing there, she declares, *"If people from our countries saw these sights, they would stop complaining about their petty troubles."*

She then joins the city of Darjeeling to continue her novitiate. At its conclusion, in 1929, she takes the religious habit, prepares to become a teacher, and then pronounces her temporary vows in May 1931, adopting the name Sister Mary Teresa, in reference to the protection sought from Saint Thérèse of Lisieux, canonized in May 1925 by Pope Pius XI.

From 1931 to 1937, Sister Teresa teaches in Calcutta, and her students quickly nickname her "Ma," which means "Mother." From then on, her nickname Mother Teresa would never leave her. Her final vows are pronounced in 1937, thus becoming "the spouse of Jesus for all eternity,"and in 1944, she becomes the director of studies at Saint Mary's, a school primarily dedicated to the upper classes of Calcutta.

However, she spends a lot of time in the slums of Calcutta helping the sick and visiting those who are already hospitalized.

It is in September 1946, on a train from Calcutta to Darjeeling, while she is unsuccessfully seeking sleep, that she receives a direct call from God. Regarding this, she stated, *"Suddenly, I heard with certainty the voice of God. The message was clear: I had to leave the convent and help the poor by living with them. It was an order, a duty, a certainty. I knew what I had to do, but I didn't know how."*

Mother Teresa keeps silent about this mystical experience and convinces herself to found a new religious order.

In 1950, she founds the Missionaries of Charity congregation in Calcutta, where the sisters dress in saris to better integrate with the Indian population. Mother Teresa then adopts her famous white sari bordered with blue, which will accompany her throughout her life.

The congregation serves the poorest of the poor and spreads to other regions of India. The friendship between Mother Teresa and the Prime Minister of Bengal allows the nun to find the introductions and financial assistance necessary for this expansion.

In 1959, Mother Teresa extends her work to Ranchi, then to New Delhi, in the presence of Prime Minister Nehru.

Then in 1965, thanks to authorization granted by Pope Paul VI, the congregation also rapidly expands to other continents, especially in Latin America. The success of this development is realized when, in 1979, Mother Teresa, then 69 years old, is awarded the Nobel Peace Prize.

Her fame is then established among the general public on the international stage. Right after that, Dominique Lapierre, co-author with the American Larry Collins of Is Paris Burning ? arrives with his wife in Calcutta at Mother Teresa's place. He donates $50,000, saying, *"It's a drop in the ocean,"* and Mother Teresa replies, *"Yes, but without them, the ocean would not be the ocean."*

In 1985, Dominique Lapierre publishes his bestseller The City of Joy, which sells 12 million copies and contributes to highlighting the role and dedication of religious figures, notably Gaston Grandjean, who assist the destitute in the slums of Calcutta.

The same year, she is honored by US President Ronald Reagan, and then she creates in New York the first shelter for the victims.

However, her fragile health always posed a challenge. In 1989, Mother Teresa suffered a heart attack and was forced to relinquish her position as head of the Missionaries of Charity.

By 1997, the religious community founded by Mother Teresa comprised 4,000 sisters, established in 610 foundations spread across 123 countries worldwide.

That same year, she met Pope John Paul II for the last time and returned to Calcutta, where she passed away a few weeks later at the age of 87.

Even beyond her death, her earthly journey was not entirely over, so to speak, as she was beatified on October 19, 2003, by Pope John Paul II and canonized on September 4, 2016, by Pope Francis.

Madeleine Cinquin was born in Brussels, Belgium, on November 16, 1908. It was much later, under her religious name **Sister Emmanuelle**, that she would become famous for her work in serving the poor.

While her mother was Belgian, her father was French, and her parents ran a fine lingerie business in the Saint Omer region. She was the second of three children. Everything went peacefully until the day she turned 6, when she witnessed her father drown before her eyes on the beach in Ostend while swimming in the sea.

In addition to the immense pain of losing her father so tragically, she felt the fragility of existence, and she later said that her religious vocation was born that day.

Under the guidance of her mother, who raised her alone but whom she later described as a strong woman, a fighter. Young Madeleine developed a strong character marked by the stamp of hardship. She had a lot of vitality, a genuine thirst for life, and a rebellious and defiant temperament.

At the age of ten, the love of God became evident to her, and at 18, when it was time for her to court boys and attend balls, as her mother encouraged her to do, she wanted to become a saint and a missionary.

Her family, who knew her as joyful and always ready to have fun, was dismayed by this eternally rebellious daughter, whom they couldn't imagine spending her life in a convent.

Madeleine paid little heed to their opinions and entered the Order of Our Lady of Sion at the age of 21, a teaching and semi-cloistered congregation founded by Alphonse de Ratisbonne in 1843.

She took her vows on May 10, 1931, and adopted the name Sister Emmanuelle, which means *"God with us"* in Hebrew.

She earned a degree in philosophical and religious sciences and taught successively in Turkey from 1932 to 1963, interrupted by a period in Tunisia between 1954 and 1959.

Then, she went to Egypt in 1964, where she taught in Alexandria among children from wealthy families, which didn't suit her.

She decided then, in 1965, to take charge of a small school for the poor and moved in with a poor family herself to be closer to their reality.

From this journey to the land of pyramids, she adopted the phrase "Yalla," which means "Forward" in Arabic and became one of her favorite expressions and the title of one of her books published in 1999 (Yalla, Forward Young People).

At 62, upon retirement, she now finds herself in Cairo, in Ezbet-El-Nakhl, a slum where rag-pickers live, who work in garbage collection and are nicknamed the "zabbalines."

She will share their lives for 22 years. In 1985, she founded the association Act, Support, Mobilize for the Future of Children, AS-MAE, which is entirely secular and helps children in need regardless of their beliefs, particularly in accessing healthcare and education.

To date, ASMAE is located in eight countries, including France, assists 39,000 beneficiaries through 24 projects, and thanks to more than 23,000 donors. She has now become"the little sister of the poor."

A feminist ahead of her time, she once said, *"Educating a man is educating an individual; educating a woman is educating a nation."*

In 1991, Egyptian President Mubarak granted her Egyptian citizenship, in tribute to her work in the country and to celebrate the"diamond jubilee"of her religious life.

In the 1990s, she gained much popularity in France by participating in the TV show La Marche du Siècle hosted by Jean-Marie Cavada, where she addressed politicians and journalists alike.

In 1995, along with Geneviève de Gaulle-Anthonioz, she inspired the theme of social fracture and exclusion that would guide Jacques Chirac's presidential campaign. Chirac awarded her the Legion of Honor's Commander's necktie in 2002, and she was later elevated to the rank of Grand Officer by Nicolas Sarkozy in 2008.

Sister Emmanuelle died in October 2008 at the age of 99, while she had retired to Notre-Dame de Sion in Callian, Var.

Belgium, her native country, also pays tribute to her. Already made a Grand Officer of the Order of the Crown in 2005, King Albert II of Belgium attended the requiem Mass in her memory at the Cathedral of Saints Michael and Gudula in Brussels.

It is possible that a beatification process may open in the future concerning her.

Mohandas Karamchand Gandhi was born on October 2, 1869, in Porbandar, Gujarat, India. He was the youngest child of his father's fourth wife. His father was a lawyer and government official belonging to a merchant caste. At that time, India was a British colony subject to English laws.

Gandhi lost his father at a young age, and according to the family traditions of the time, he was married at the age of 13 to a girl of his own age, Kasturba. She bore him four sons. In 1888, Gandhi went to England, to London, to study law for three years, and he proved to be a diligent student and adhered to a modest lifestyle. He loved literature and philosophy, and was particularly interested in Leo Tolstoy, John Ruskin, and Henry David Thoreau. He became a lawyer in 1891 and briefly joined the High Court of Justice in London. Returning to India, to Bombay, he failed to practice law due to his unfamiliarity with Indian laws and eventually returned to his hometown, Porbandar.

Fortunately, an employment opportunity arose for him quite quickly, leading him to go to South Africa, to Durban. While traveling to Pretoria on a business trip by train, he was traveling first class with a regularly purchased ticket and discovered racism when a white passenger, aided by train conductors and police, forcibly ejected him from the train.

This episode marked him for life, especially since the next day, a similar incident occurred to him on a stagecoach he took to Johannesburg. Later, he was assaulted by a police officer on duty for simply being in the street after 9 pm.

These various incidents sparked a desire to act against the oppression of Indians in South Africa, especially as discriminatory laws against them were passed in 1894 and 1895.

 Over time, Gandhi became a political leader representing the Indian community in South Africa, particularly in the coastal province of Natal, starting in 1896. He was 27 years old at the time. Promoting this cause even in his homeland, India, Gandhi began to annoy the British authorities, especially because of articles, interviews, or meetings authored by him defending the Indian cause in South Africa.

His writings, distorted and exaggerated, became popularly known as the Green Pamphlet and worried the European community. During a quarantine at the Durban port of the ship on which Gandhi was aboard, members of this community threatened to drown all the ship's passengers. However, Gandhi refused to testify against the attackers.

In 1899, during the Second Boer War, Gandhi supported the Boers who were fighting for their independence, while recommending that the Indian community support the British authorities. He helped establish a corps of 1100 volunteer ambulance workers.

Gandhi was influenced by his readings of religious books, which encouraged him to follow and practice concepts of non-possession, equality, and communal living. He became a proponent of sexual abstinence (Brahmacharya in Indian), possibly influenced in this regard by John Ruskin, whose marriage to his companion Effie Gray was annulled for non-consummation.

Gandhi also became a vegetarian, consuming almost exclusively dried and fresh fruits, all of which supported the concept called Satyagraha, which is a path of purification of one's life and passive resistance based on true strength.

Gandhi implemented this strategy of non-violence from 1907 to oppose a law (the Black Act) on the registration of Asians in South Africa.

Gandhi was arrested and imprisoned several times while demanding the repeal or amendment of this law. Then, in late 1913, he led a march between the Natal colony and the Transvaal to protest against an immigrant law (the Immigrants Regulation Act of 1913). This march marked a milestone in South Africa's history.

After spending over twenty years in South Africa fighting discrimination, Gandhi returned to India in 1914, not without making a detour to England to establish a new Indian ambulance corps and assist the British army engaged in World War I.

In April 1919, Indian troops under British command fired on protesters, including women and children, in a garden in Amritsar, Punjab. The massacre resulted in between 400 and 1500 deaths according to various estimates. Gandhi's response was very measured: he called for calm and non-violence, which earned him the hatred of Sikh and Hindu extremists.

Upon his return to India, Gandhi earned his honorary title of Mahatma, meaning "Great Soul," as millions of Indian peasants regarded him as a true saint.

Gandhi joined the Indian National Congress, a rather moderate party, taking control of it in 1920.

In January 1930, the Indian National Congress declared India's independence, a declaration not recognized by the British, who then engaged in negotiations. In March of the same year, Gandhi launched a non-violent march against a British tax on salt. This march, which lasted for a month,

Over nearly 400 kilometers, Gandhi's march will make him very popular beyond India itself, drawing huge crowds along his route. Gandhi is then 61 years old.

In response to this salt march, the British authorities will imprison between 60,000 and 90,000 people, but eventually in 1931, the British government releases all detainees and signs the Gandhi-Irwin Pact, which invites Gandhi to official negotiations in London as the sole representative of the Indian National Congress.

The negotiations fail and even make Gandhi a personal enemy of Winston Churchill, who considers him one of the worst threats to the British Empire, even nicknaming him the Indian Mussolini.

In 1934, Gandhi resigns from the Indian National Congress and resumes political activity two years later, in 1936 under Nehru's presidency.

During the Second World War, Gandhi opposes any Indian participation in the conflict, which once again leads to his imprisonment. Gandhi indeed believes that India had no reason to fight for the defense of democratic ideals, while these same ideals were denied to the Indian nation.

Despite Gandhi's stance, nearly two and a half million Indians will fight under the British flag during this world conflict.

In 1942, at the age of 73, Gandhi calls for non-cooperation with the British Empire, but also for non-violence towards British subjects, even if they commit acts of violence.

In 1944, Gandhi, again in prison, falls victim to a malaria attack. He is released for health reasons and then engages in the Indian Muslim League, aiming to unite Muslims and non-Muslims in India.

At the end of the Second World War, Gandhi rejects a partition of India along religious lines and demands the departure of the British from India. The Muslim League is divided on the partition issue and demands the formation of Muslim and non-Muslim states.

A day of action in 1946 results in new massacres of thousands of Hindus and Muslims.

In August 1947, Gandhi and Muslim leader Muhammad Jinnah find common ground with the British, represented by Lord Mountbatten, on the principle of Indian independence, but the two leaders remain divided on the partition.

The religious tensions led to the secession of Pakistan, a partition that resulted in over 500,000 deaths in religious riots.

On January 30, 1948, in New Delhi, while Gandhi was on his way to a prayer gathering, he was shot three times by a Hindu nationalist extremist. Over a million people attended his funeral. Gandhi died at the age of 78 and remains a towering figure in both Indian and global history of the 20th century.

One of the best Gandhi's quote was, *"Strength does not come from physical capacity. it comes from an indomitable will."*

To conclude this chapter, let's talk about **Moses**, whose existence, believer or non-believer, cannot be proven. According to the biblical text, it was when Moses reached the age of 80 that God revealed himself to him in a burning bush and assigned him the mission of leading the "Children of Israel"out of Egypt to free them from slavery.

Moses died at the age of 120.

WAY NUMBER TWENTY FOUR

WAY NUMBER TWENTY-FOUR : BLOWING OUT THE CANDLES

Jeanne Louise Calment was born on February 21, 1875, in Arles, on Rue du Roure. At that time, the life expectancy for women did not exceed 45 years.

Her father, Nicolas, was a shipbuilder, and her mother came from a family of millers. She had an older brother who would live to be 97 years old.

As her family was relatively well-off, she had the opportunity, uncommon for her time, to attend school until she was sixteen. She also took cooking, decorative art, and dance classes, and she obtained her diploma.

At the age of 13, she met Vincent Van Gogh, who came to buy canvas for his paintings at the family shop. She later said of him that he was as ugly as a louse, more interested in drinking than painting, and that the prostitutes, although frightened by his appearance, liked him because he paid well. She nicknamed him -*"the crazy one,"* -with a face ravaged by alcohol.

She married her first cousin, Fernand Calment, in 1896. He was 27 years old and a wealthy draper. They moved to Rue Gambetta in Arles, into an apartment above their store, simply called -*"Grand Magasin Calment."* They soon had a daughter named Yvonne, born in 1898, who would be Jeanne's only child.

Jeanne started smoking cigarettes, influenced by her husband. She remained faithful to Fernand throughout her life.

Her father died in January 1931, and her daughter Yvonne died in 1934 at the age of 36 from tuberculosis.

She first saw the Eiffel Tower in Paris at the age of 67 during a visit to the city.

In 1942, her husband died of food poisoning from cherries contaminated with a chemical. Jeanne would outlive him by 55 years.

In 1965, Jeanne Calment sold her apartment on a viager basis to a 45-year-old notary named André-François Raffray for 2,500 francs per month. Raffray thought it was a good deal since the seller was already 90 years old and a smoker, a habit she would keep almost her entire life.

The deal turned out to be the worst he could have made, as Raffray passed away in 1995 after having already paid twice the commercial value of the property. But it didn't end there, as it was Raffray's heirs who had to take over and pay the viager to Jeanne Calment for an additional 32 years-!

What was the secret to such longevity-? Of course, besides genetics, firstly she never had to work her entire life and even received help at home for certain household chores. She had a rich and active social life and attended many dances because she loved to dance.

Her diet was far from exemplary. Besides cigarettes, she enjoyed good food, wine, meat, cakes, but all in moderation. She regularly consumed olive oil, skipped breakfasts, slept well, and took naps. She enjoyed sports activities, started fencing at the age of 85, and rode a bike until she was 100 years old.

She meditated, prayed, regularly attended church, and avoided using heating in winter. She never took any medication.

During the harsh winter of 1985 in Arles, Jeanne Calment, then 110 years old, moved to the Lac retirement home.

The following year, in 1986, Jeanne Calment became the new oldest living French person after the death of the previous record holder, a certain Eugénie Roux. She then made her first television appearances.

It was especially from 1988 that her fame became international. She was first invited to meet journalists on the occasion of the centenary of Vincent Van Gogh's visit to Arles.

In 1989, she begins to become a phenomenon of longevity and attracts continual media attention. She appears in the film *Vincent and Me* by Michael Rubbio in 1990, playing herself in relation to Vincent Van Gogh.

In 1991, she becomes the world's oldest living person and definitively enters the Guinness World Records in 1993 as the oldest person in the world.

In October 1995, Jeanne Calment, now 120 years and 238 days old, breaks all records for longevity ever recorded, both for men and women. In 1996, she speaks on a CD and mentions rap.

On August 4, 1997, the grim reaper finally arrives and takes Jeanne at the age of 122 years, 5 months, and 14 days, while several scientific studies show that there seems to be a kind of glass ceiling in human longevity, around 116 years for women.

At her death, tributes pour in from both the Mayor of Arles, Michel Vauzelle, and the President of the French Republic, Jacques Chirac, as well as from his cohabitation Prime Minister, Lionel Jospin.

Her funeral takes place in strict privacy at the cemetery of Arles.

As for the male side, one must turn to Japan, which surprises no one given the very particular age pyramid of this country.

Jiroemon Kimura was born in April 1897 in Kyoto, the same year as the fire at the Bazar de la Charité in Paris, which killed 125 people, mostly women from the Parisian high aristocracy.

In the early 1900s, he attended primary school, which he finished at the age of 14, then found a job as a telegraph operator in a post office in Nakahama, a locality near Kyoto.

He would now work his entire life in a post office until retirement age, then he would help his son, a farmer, until he was 90 years old.

He had some interruptions in this long postal career, notably during the First World War, during which he served in a unit of the Japanese Imperial Army in charge of military communications. He also briefly went to Korea in 1920, then married his neighbor Yae Kimura the same year, with whom he remained faithful for his entire life. She gave him six sons and two daughters.

Jiroemon survived the 1927 earthquake that struck Tokyo and its region, claiming several thousand lives. He mentioned this fact in a statement he released on the occasion of his 114th birthday in 2011.

Once retired, he helped his son with agricultural work and his son's entrepreneurial projects.

His lifestyle was spartan and disciplined-; he woke up at dawn, ate sparingly and in small portions. He read newspapers daily and enjoyed listening to parliamentary debates on television. Apparently, this lifestyle suited him well as Kimura never fell ill, even though his eyesight declined.

In 2012, the Guinness World Records issued a certificate to Kimura as a verified super centenarian, and in 2013, the same Guinness recognized him as the world's oldest man and the oldest living person. In 2016, Kimura passed away from pneumonia at the age of 116 years and 54 days. He was the first man to officially celebrate his 116th birthday.

He had lived through the entire 20th century and its many upheavals, including those involving his country during the Second World War, without the tranquility of his peaceful existence being affected.

On his 116th birthday, the then Prime Minister of Japan, Shinzō Abe, who would be assassinated in 2022, sent him a congratulatory video message.

When asked by a Bloomberg journalist about his longevity, he replied, *"I eat light to live long."*

During his long life, Jiroemon had the time to have eight children, 14 grandchildren, 25 great-grandchildren, and 13 great-great-grandchildren.

WAY NUMBER TWENTY FIVE

WAY NUMBER TWENTY-FIVE : BREAK THE BANK

Theodore Struyck, known as "Théo," had a one in 292 million chances of winning a jackpot in the American Powerball, one of the most popular national lotteries with no ceiling limit.

And perhaps even less chance of winning one of the biggest jackpots of that lottery on that day, namely one billion seven hundred sixty-five million dollars.

In principle, when a player wins such an amount, they have only one obsession, preserving their anonymity, if only for security reasons.

But here's the thing: Théo played in California, and Californian law doesn't allow claiming the prize anonymously, forcing Théo to step out of the shadows. We learned that he adored children, was highly regarded by his neighbors, purchased his winning ticket at a local grocery store where he regularly went, and owned a small boat to indulge in his favorite pastime, fishing.

For him, big-game fishing has just become miraculous! And winning such a sum at 65 years old promises a retirement that looks like the birth of a new life.

Gloria Mackenzie was 84 years old when she won $590.5 million on May 18, 2013, in the Powerball, one of the two major American lotteries along with Mega Millions.

She then became the biggest winner of that age in the entire United States.

Married in 1951, she lived before her win in a mobile home near the town of Paco in Florida, relying on Social Security pensions.

Since gambling winnings are taxed in the United States, she was left with"only" $278 million after taxes. Based in Florida, the elderly lady bought the winning ticket when someone agreed to let her go ahead in line.

She shared her fabulous winnings with her son Scott, an assistant manager in a shoe store, who later claimed to have paid her half of the ticket, which amounted to five dollars.

She bought a house of about 1500 square meters worth just over 1 million dollars, making her daughter the heir. Instead of hiring an army of servants, she preferred to rely on the care of her family, especially her son.

As Gloria wasn't sure how to manage this fortune, she entrusted her son with it, and he swore to take care of her until the end of her days.

The problem is that the son didn't have many more ideas than his mother about what to do with the mountain of dollars, so he relied on the sound advice of a tax advisor, Harry "Hank"Madden, who provided his tax recommendations every Saturday morning on a local radio station.

In doing so, Scott made a serious mistake by not seeking the advice of a nationally or even internationally renowned tax firm, especially considering that Harry Madden had never had the opportunity to handle such large sums, and that he had previously been fired from an investment firm for fund manipulation.

Instead of prioritizing investments that yield returns, the advisor and the son squander the funds by investing in operations and trusts without interest. The"advisor"also charges the old lady an additional $2 million in fees without any justification.

Since the son has power of attorney to manage his mother's affairs, he can act as he pleases and even goes so far as to eject her from the home they shared on the grounds that he no longer had the capacity to care for her. She then goes to live in Jacksonville with another one of her children.

At the age of 90, Gloria Mackenzie then files a lawsuit against her son Scott for negligence, misinformation, and breach of fiduciary duty. She also complains that her son took advantage of her to enrich himself and engaged in abuse of weakness against her.

In his defense, the son claims that he merely introduced his mother to Harry"Hank" Madden and is not responsible for what followed. As for personal enrichment, he attributes it to the $5 he gave his mother to buy the ticket, which entitled him to claim 50% of the initial winnings. This point was never really proven.

The amount of the winnings should have generated tens of millions of dollars in interest if it had been properly invested.

Gloria dies in February 2021 in her home at the Glen Kernan Country Club in Florida, without the lawsuit reaching a final resolution.

Dennis Banfield, in a similar vein to Gloria Mackenzie but in a much happier way, is British.

Having served in the military in Holland, Germany, and Italy, he served in the Royal Air Force in Egypt.

Afterward, he worked for 40 years at the South West Electricity Board and lived for 57 years in the same small house they owned in Bristol with his wife Shirley.

Shirley worked most of her life as a local government employee and a commercial assistant shortly before retiring.

Dennis is 87 years old and Shirley is 83 when Dennis buys a Lucky Dip lottery ticket in 2018 at a kiosk near their home for £2, against his wife's advice, tired of seeing him always lose.

The next day, glancing at the winning numbers in a newspaper, she casually says to Dennis, *"Who could possibly have those numbers ?"* and Dennis replies, *"I do." He also says, "Winning is just a matter of time."*

The win is substantial: £18 million, and Dennis becomes Britain's oldest major winner. Dennis has been playing from the start with the aim of providing financial security for his two daughters.

After the complete shock of discovering the win, his wife Shirley said the couple was considering replacing their old three-door Nissan Micra with something a bit more comfortable, but certainly not a Ferrari or a Maserati.

Dennis, suffering from a leg infection that required hospitalization, says he may need a driver to drive their car.

She also said that she and her husband would share the jackpot with their two daughters, Tina and Karen, aged 54 and 51 respectively at the time of the win.

Dennis's passion is carving wooden Nativity figures for his local church's nativity scene.

His latest work was a cradle measuring 6 feet long, 1m high, and 1m deep, intended for the church's nativity scene in Winterbourne near Bristol.

WAY NUMBER TWENTY SIX

WAY NUMBER TWENTY-SIX : PLAYING SOLITAIRE

Francis Charles Chichester was born on September 17, 1901, in Barnstaple, Devon, England. He was the second son of an Anglican pastor who didn't particularly like him. He was nearsighted, and his childhood was joyless. However, from a young age, he was already passionate about aviation and navigation. During World War I, he attended Marlborough College, a public school founded in 1843 for the children of the Anglican Church clergy.

At 18, he left England for New Zealand, where he took on various jobs such as miner, salesman, and land agent, eventually becoming interested in aviation while also improving his knowledge of sailing navigation. His businesses then collapsed due to the Great Depression.

Returning to England, he founded an airline in which he himself was a pilot. At the age of 30, he made his first solo flight between Europe and Australia, taking 40 days to cover the 21,000 miles separating the two destinations.

In 1931, he became the first aviator to fly solo across the Tasman Sea between New Zealand and Australia, in a de Havilland Gipsy Moth plane equipped with floats.

During World War II, he wrote navigation instruction manuals for army pilots that did not require the use of maps. However, at the end of the war, he founded a successful mapping company.

In 1958, at the age of 57, Chichester was diagnosed with lung cancer, which his wife treated in her own way through a strict vegetarian diet. While doctors wanted to remove one of his lungs, giving him a life expectancy of six months, fruits and vegetables worked a miracle on Chichester's body, and he went into remission.

In 1960, Chichester made his first solo transatlantic crossing aboard the Gipsy Moth III. He covered the route from Plymouth to New York in 40 days, finishing first in this English transatlantic race, and explained that this race was part of the healing process for his cancer.

In 1964, he finished second in another transatlantic race, just behind Éric Tabarly.

At the age of over 65, he accomplished the feat that would definitively make him famous worldwide. He embarked on the Gipsy Moth IV for a solo circumnavigation of the globe. The Gipsy was normally designed for a crew of eight.

Setting off alone from Plymouth on August 27, 1966, he covered 14,100 miles in one go to reach Sydney, Australia. He set off again two days later and returned to Plymouth via Cape Horn, this time covering 15,517 miles in just 119 days, the longest distance ever covered solo on a small sailboat without any stops, and also the fastest.

His main navigation instruments were a sextant and a Rolex Oyster Perpetual chronometer. At Cape Horn, he faced winds of 185km/h and waves of 15 meters.

His return was triumphant, and he became a hero: to welcome

him, 250,000 people crowded the quays of Plymouth, and 300 boats accompanied him on the final miles.

One of his best quote was:" *Any damn fool can navigate the world sober. It takes a really good sailor to do it drunk.*"

Queen Elizabeth II knighted him in May 1967 with a sword that had belonged to Sir Francis Drake, making him a Commander of the Order of the British Empire.

Now entitled to the title of Sir, Sir Francis Chichester took the helm again and made one last solo crossing between Portuguese Guinea and Nicaragua in January-February 1971.

Then in 1972, he attempted another English transatlantic race on Gipsy Moth IV but had to abandon off the coast of Spain. The "crab" had indeed caught up with him, and his wife, now powerless against the progress of the disease, saw her husband succumb to lung cancer in August 1972.

Chichester died forever glorified, and he would be the subject of a song dedicated to his memory by the rock band Dire Straits, titled "Single-Handed Sailor."

Alejandra Rodriguez won the title of Miss Universe Buenos Aires on April 25, 2024, and will represent Argentina in the upcoming international edition of the competition in the fall of 2024. However, while she made headlines in the international press following this designation, it was not so much for the title itself, but because Alejandra is 60 years old.

Despite her age, she remains a very beautiful woman with a sharp mind, as she is a professional lawyer and journalist.

Her participation in the Miss Universe competition became possible after the organizing committee of this prestigious competition recently lifted the age limits that had been in place for 70 years, which required candidates to be between 18 and 28 years old.

Alejandra stated, *"Women are not only physical beauty but another set of values."* She is enthusiastic about representing this new paradigm in beauty pageants. Alejandra was preferred during her selection in Buenos Aires over 34 other contestants, whose ages ranged from 18 to 73 years old.

CHAPTER 30

WAY NUMBER TWENTY SEVEN

WAY NUMBER TWENTY-SEVEN : BEING CLOSE TO A CELEBRITY

René Angélil was born in Canada on January 16, 1942.

His father hailed from Damascus, Syria, and his mother, Alice Sara, was a Canadian of Syrian-Lebanese descent.

René began a singing career in the early 1960s in a Canadian trio, Les Baronets, with two other Quebecois singers, Pierre Labelle and Jean Beaulne. Their first record was called *"Johanne"* and was part of the yéyé wave of that time. The trio enjoyed some success, performing all over the province of Quebec and especially in the bars and cabarets of Montreal.

Interpreting songs by the Beatles or American rock hits, things could have continued this way, but in 1966 their record label went bankrupt, and then the trio began to disintegrate. Jean Beaulne left the trio in 1966, was replaced in 1967, and the group became Les Nouveaux Baronets.

In 1972, the group disbanded, with René Angélil and Pierre La-belle each becoming artist managers or impresarios. Throughout the 1960s, the trio made a name for themselves, but their fame was limited to"la belle province" (Quebec).

From 1966 to 1972, René Angélil was in a relationship with Denyse Duquette, with whom he had a son, Patrick. After divorcing Denyse in 1972, René quickly found a new partner, the popular singer Anne Renée, whom he married, and who gave him a son and a daughter.

René also dabbled in cinema, playing roles in some comedies, including Après ski in 1971.

He was also a poker enthusiast, and over the years, he became a professional in the discipline to the point of qualifying for the championship series in 2005.

As a talent manager, René Angélil began to represent the singer and actress Ginette Raynault, whose stage name is Ginette Reno. She is a renowned singer with a considerable discography and performs in the largest Canadian and international venues.

However, despite a success story-like career, Ginette Reno decided to part ways with René Angélil, prompting him for a while to leave the talent management profession.

In 1981, at the age of 39, René Angélil listened to a song by a young 13-year-old girl, Céline Dion, titled Ce n'était qu'un rêve, a song written by her mother and brother. The song received immediate success in Quebec, and René Angélil was impressed by the beauty of this young voice.

He then decided to take care of the singer's career, who recorded a series of French-language songs, including the title *D'amour ou d'amitié* in 1983, which launched her career in France. She was only 15 years old at the time.

In 1984, René also took charge of the singing career of Claudette Dion, who was 20 years older than her sister Céline.

In 1988, Céline Dion won the Eurovision Song Contest in Dublin, representing Switzerland in front of 600 million of viewers.

René Angélil's talent management career flourished in the 1980s, as he not only managed Céline Dion but also his second wife Anne Renée, as well as Quebec artists like Véronique Béliveau, Johnny Farago, and René Simard.

Céline, who learned English, achieved success after success, and in 1990, her English-language album Unison propelled her to the status of a pop artist who made a mark in the North American and Anglo-Saxon markets.

Then, while still in her twenties, two albums, *Falling into You* in 1996 and *Let's Talk About Love* in 1997, each sold over 30 million copies and became among the best-selling albums in the world.

On December 17, 1994, at the age of 52, René Angélil married Céline Dion, who was 26, in the Notre-Dame Basilica of Montreal, a highly publicized wedding, spiced up by the age difference between the two spouses and Céline's fame, which reflected on René.

In 1997, Céline recorded one of her greatest hits with the song *My Heart Will Go On*, featured in James Cameron's film Titanic.

Behind each of Céline's successes lies the work and support of her now-husband, René Angélil.

In 1999, René Angélil successfully underwent treatment for throat cancer.

In January 2001, Céline and René welcomed their first child, René-Charles, conceived through assisted reproductive technology (ART). René, already the father of three children from his two previous marriages, became a father again at the age of 59.

From 2005 to 2007, René excelled in poker competitions, and rumors said he was betting a million dollars per week at Caesars Palace in Las Vegas and a similar amount in another Vegas casino, the Bellagio.

In October 2010, at the age of 68, René became a father again, welcoming twins, Eddy and Nelson, with Céline, also through assisted reproductive technology. Céline had suffered a miscarriage in 2009.

Cancer caught up with René again at the end of 2013, once more in his throat, and he had to undergo surgery to remove a tumor. A year later, in 2014, René could no longer manage Céline's career due to health reasons.

The respite was short-lived, as René Angélil was eventually taken by his cancer on January 14, 2016, in Las Vegas, just two days before his 74th birthday.

Thomas Wayne Markle was born on July 18, 1944, in Newport, Pennsylvania, on the east coast of the United States.

In the 1970s, Markle worked as a lighting director at a Chicago television station, WTTW. His work was recognized in 1975 when he was awarded a local Emmy Award by The Chicago/Midwest Emmy Awards for his lighting design for TV series.

In 1982, he was nominated for a Daytime Emmy Award, which honors artistic and technical achievements within the American television industry. In 1984, he supervised the lighting for the Los Angeles Olympics.

In 1986 and 2001, he continued to receive similar awards from the industry for his work as a lighting designer on various TV series. In short, Thomas Markle is an excellent lighting designer, but he would have remained largely unknown to the general public, except for professionals in the American television industry, if he weren't also the father of Rachel Meghan, born in August 1981 when he was 37 years old.

Thomas separated from Meghan's mother in 1983, divorced in 1987, and took full custody of his daughter when she was nine, allowing her mother, Doria, to focus fully on her professional career.

Thomas paid for his daughter's education from elementary school to university, which she completed at Northwestern University in Illinois. Her acting career followed, and she began appearing in American TV series. She married a film producer in 2011, from whom she divorced in 2014.

In 2016, Thomas found himself unable to settle a thirty-thousand-dollar debt.

It was in 2018, when the whole world would hear about Thomas Markle, at the age of 74.

Meghan was to become the Duchess of Sussex through her marriage at Windsor Castle to Prince Harry, the younger son of Prince Charles and Lady Diana Spencer.

The international press wondered if Meghan's father would attend the ceremony with his daughter, knowing that he was not welcome in Windsor.

Indeed, a few days earlier, the press revealed that he had negotiated photos, with Meghan's agreement, to earn money from the media attention on his daughter.

This information displeased Buckingham Palace, even though Markle later explained that the photos were published without his consent. He filed lawsuits and demanded one million dollars in damages from the photo agency Coleman-Rayner in a Los Angeles court.

Later, Thomas became estranged from his daughter, explaining that without him, she was nothing and would never have become the Duchess of Sussex.

Thomas Markle did not attend his daughter's wedding, first claiming that he was recovering from heart surgery, even though he was discharged from the hospital two days before the ceremony.

Later, he claimed that he never received an official invitation.

In the 2020s and beyond, he alternates between legal proceedings and sensational statements against his daughter and Harry, explaining that Meghan only wanted to become a duchess for the money and that she and Harry have dishonored the British Crown and lost their souls.

Jamie Parnell Spears was born in Kentwood, Louisiana in 1952. His younger brother, Austin, died three days after birth, which plunged his mother into despair. She made three suicide attempts during Jamie's early childhood, but this did not affect his schooling, which proceeded without incident.

Unfortunately, when he was 14, his mother went to the cemetery where Austin was buried and shot herself in the chest on her son's grave.

Later, at the age of 17, Jamie survived a car accident that killed a member of his football team who was with him.

In the mid-1970s, Jamie worked as a boilermaker-welder, then ventured into real estate development and built his own fitness center with a spa. Later, he owned a seafood restaurant called Granny's.

After his first marriage to Debbie Sanders Cross, Jamie remarried Lynne Irene Bridges in 1976, a marriage that lasted 26 years, even though they had considered divorce as early as the 1980s due to Jamie's alcoholism issues, which he battled for a long time until undergoing detoxification in 2004.

This union brought them three children : Bryan in 1977, Britney in 1981, and Jamie Lynn in 1991.

Britney and her mother Lynne attended auditions and shows together as the young singer's career took off. It was especially in the late 1990s and early 2000s that Britney became a true icon of "teen pop music," selling over 150 million records worldwide.

In 2008, Jamie Spears obtained conservatorship over his daughter Britney, then 27, regarding her personal life and finances. This decision was made after the pop singer's public mental health issues.

Indeed, Britney began to make tabloid headlines for certain

strange behaviors, including attacking a photographer's car with an umbrella.

After her split from her husband, Kevin Federline, Britney began a downward spiral. Her career was at a standstill, and her life became a succession of scandals that delighted paparazzi, involving heavy partying, substance abuse, car accidents, and bizarre attire, such as when she shaved her head completely in front of cameras in 2007.

After several stays in psychiatric facilities, Britney loses custody of her two sons from her marriage to Federline, and Jamie's temporary conservatorship over his daughter, which had been temporary, becomes permanent.

Starting in 2009, a movement of Britney fans organizes on the internet, which becomes the *"Free Britney movement"* to end Jamie's conservatorship over Britney. But it is really from 2019 onwards that this movement will become widely known and popular and thrust Jamie both into the spotlight and under media scrutiny, at the age of 67.

The movement in support of Britney receives numerous endorsements from celebrities such as Paris Hilton, Cher, Miley Cyrus, as well as organizations like the American Civil Liberties Union, which has nearly 2 million members.

In August 2020, Jamie Spears dismisses the #FreeBritney movement as a "joke" and its organizers as "conspiracy theorists."

Britney responds with legal actions to change the terms of the conservatorship and to substitute her manager, Jodi Montgomery, for her father in the conservatorship role.

The legal controversy continues until November 2021, when a judge terminates the conservatorship, despite Britney's ex-husband, Kevin Federline, stating that he was 100% convinced that the conservatorship had saved Britney's life.

Starting in 2018, Jamie Spears' health began to seriously decline, with a severe colon rupture, followed in 2023 by a leg amputation due to an infection, which now requires him to use a wheelchair for mobility.

As for Britney, she has stated that she sees no reason to reconcile with a father she described as abusive in a Los Angeles court in June 2021, and she has published details of the 13 years of conservatorship imposed on her and its impact on her personal life in a book titled The Woman in Me.

Mohamed Al-Fayed, recently deceased at the age of 94, although already known in business circles after his acquisition of the Ritz hotel in Paris in 1979 and London department store Harrods in 1985, is still far from being an international celebrity. He immediately ascends to this status in 1997, at the age of 68, when his son Dodi, then the boyfriend of Princess Diana, dies with her in a car crash in a tunnel under the Pont de l'Alma.

From then on, Mohamed Al-Fayed suggests that the two lovers were murdered on the orders of the British Crown to cover up the scandal, even as the princess may have been pregnant with Dodi at the time.

Dodi himself gained worldwide fame when his romantic relationship with Lady Diana was revealed in 1997 thanks to photos published by the tabloids showing their vacation in Saint-Tropez on a luxury yacht.

In general, the tabloid press, and social media are always interested in the parental history of international stars. This includes Jane and William Alvin Pitt, parents of **Brad Pitt,** Tina Knowles, mother of **Beyoncé**, George Paul **DiCaprio**, father of **Leonardo**, or John Voight, an actor already known for Deliverance and Midnight Cowboy, but especially father to **Angelina Jolie.**

WAY NUMBER TWENTY EIGHT

WAY NUMBER TWENTY-EIGHT: BECOMING KNOWN AF-TER DEATH

Paul Cézanne is now considered one of the most important Post-Impressionist painters of the 19th century, with some of his paintings fetching prices at auction of up to 50 million euros.

Born on January 19, 1839, in Aix-en-Provence, Paul Cézanne only began painting in 1860 in his hometown. His father, Louis-Auguste, was a hat maker, from a very modest background, and ran a shop on the Cours Mirabeau. His mother, Anne, was a hat maker. Later, Louis-Auguste became a banker and was able to provide relative comfort to his family, allowing Paul to attend primary and secondary school in establishments where he became friends with Émile Zola, the future astronomer Jean-Baptistin Baille, and a future lawyer, Louis-Marguery. The three friends were quickly nicknamed "the Inseparables."

Paul graduated from the Collège Bourbon in 1858 with a bachelor's degree in letters, obtained with a good mention.

As early as 1857, Paul began studying drawing at the Aix-en-Provence School of Drawing, and he was awarded a second prize in painting in 1859.

Cézanne was athletic, rather tall, but afflicted with crippling shyness and a hypersensitive nature. His Aixois accent was very pronounced.

His father, Louis-Auguste, wanted him to stay in Aix to finish his law studies and work in his bank, but this prospect plunged Paul into a state of withdrawal, leading Louis-Auguste to agree in 1861 to let his son go to Paris and join his friend Émile Zola.

Upon arriving in Paris, Cézanne tried twice to enter the École des Beaux-Arts but failed each time. He then perfected his skills on his own by frequently visiting the Louvre Museum, where he practiced copying works by Titian, Rubens, and Michelangelo.

He also attended the Académie Suisse, where he could draw live models for a very low subscription fee, allowing him to meet other artists such as Camille Pissarro, Claude Monet, and Auguste Renoir.

His early works, more focused on color than on the accuracy of forms, did not find favor with art critics and competition juries, who were attached to the predominant academic style. Cézanne fell under the influence of Gustave Courbet and Eugène Delacroix, who aimed to paint a different reality. In 1866, his Portrait of a Man presented at the Salon de Peinture et de Sculpture was rejected. From 1863, other artists such as Manet, Pissarro, and Monet, also rejected by the Salon de Paris, were exhibited at the "Salon des Refusés," authorized by Napoleon III.

In 1870, Paul Cézanne went to the south of France, to L'Estaque, to avoid military service, was influenced by the work of the young Impressionist Pissarro, and marveled at the light and colors of Provence. He also settled with Hortense Fiquet, a model and worker soon nicknamed "La Boule."

Then, in 1872, he joined Pissarro in Pontoise and worked along-side him. He also became the father of a son, Paul, born from his relationship with Hortense, whom he would subsequently paint in nearly 45 portraits. In 1874, Pissarro painted a portrait of Cézanne, with engravings of Adolphe Thiers and Gustave Courbet in the background, as a prediction that soon Cézanne too would achieve fame.

Also in 1874, the first exhibition of the Impressionist painters took place at the photographer Nadar's studio. Cézanne exhibited three paintings there, which received only negative criticism from the public. Under Pissarro's influence, he abandoned the rather dark palettes of his early works for much brighter tones, including the Grandes Baigneuses, begun in 1874-1875.

From the mid-1870s onwards, Cézanne's inspiration, blending products of his imagination and natural scenes, led him to paint more subtly, with gradations of colors and brushstrokes, to create dimension in his objects. For example, Still Life with Apples, not only depicts objects such as apples, a jug, or a jar but also conveys a sensation through the light and space rendered by the artist.

In Paris, Cézanne painted Madame Cézanne in a Blue Dress, a masterpiece of blue, green, and blue-green tones.

In the early 1880s, Cézanne painted landscapes of the surroundings of his beloved city of Aix-en-Provence and of L'Estaque near Marseille. This included the beginning of his series on Montagne Sainte-Victoire in 1887 and The Gulf of Marseille Seen from L'Estaque in 1886. Also in 1882, Cézanne was admitted to the Salon and continued to paint numerous still lifes.

He was admitted to the French Art Exhibition during the 1889 World's Fair but began to suffer severe diabetes crises the following year, diagnosed in 1890.

It was not until the age of 56, in 1895, that Paul Cézanne had his first solo exhibition in a Parisian gallery, the Vollard Gallery, although his reputation had not yet spread beyond a small circle of admirers.

Cézanne found one of his most fervent supporters in his friend Émile Zola, who wrote an article in his favor at the Salon.

Around 1899, Cézanne's reputation began to rise, but the profits did not really accrue to him because they were largely preempted by the Vollard Gallery, which bought the paintings of Renoir, Degas, Cézanne, or Van Gogh at low prices.

From 1900, Cézanne moved into his house in Aix-en-Provence and had his studio built in Les Lauves, north of Aix, where he painted from 1902 until his death. However, diabetes and various pathologies, including depression and migraines, undermined him, kept him away from his friends and the artistic community, and prevented him from working normally.

In October 1906, while Cézanne was painting the Sainte-Victoire massif again, he fell ill and died a few days later from pneumonia, at the age of 67. He left behind more than 900 paintings and 400 watercolors, some of which were unfinished.

Cézanne remained largely misunderstood during his lifetime, even vilified. Salvador Dali said of Cézanne : *"The worst painter in France is called Paul Cézanne, he is the most clumsy, the most catastrophic, the one who plunged modern art into the shit that is engulfing us."*

It was posthumously that the fame of Paul Cézanne became national, then worldwide, notably through posthumous exhibitions at the Bernheim-Jeune Gallery and at the Salon d'Automne in 1907.

The exhibition at the Salon d'Automne of 56 works by Cézanne exerted a considerable influence on subsequent painters who would illustrate Cubism, Post-Cubism, and Expressionism.

In this line of cursed artists, one cannot overlook the case of **Paul Gauguin.**

He was born in Paris, in the second arrondissement, on June 7,

1848. He was the son of Clovis Gauguin, a journalist, and Alina Maria Chazal, the daughter of a socialist feminist, Flora Tristan.

The Gauguin family left Paris for Lima, Peru, to escape the political climate following Louis-Napoléon Bonaparte's coup d'État on December 2, 1851, which drastically restricted public liberties.

During the transatlantic journey, Clovis fell ill and died. For the next four years, Paul, his sister, and their mother lived with acquaintances in Lima.

The family returned to France in 1855 and settled in Orléans, at Paul's grandfather's house. Paul completed his studies and military service in the navy, where he participated in the war of 1870. Then, in 1872, he became a stockbroker at the Paris Stock Exchange and did reasonably well.

Since his mother had died in 1867, Paul lived with his guardian, Gustave Arosa, a wealthy art collector, who introduced him to the works of Romantic painters, realists like Gustave Courbet or Jean-Baptiste-Camille Corot, and the pre-Impressionists of the Barbizon school.

In 1873, Gauguin married a Danish woman, Mette-Sophie Gad, with whom he had five children. Initially settled in Paris in the 15th arrondissement, Gauguin was an art collector and managed, with modest means, to acquire some works by Renoir, Monet, and Pissarro.

He began painting in an Impressionist style in his spare time, became acquainted with Camille Pissarro, and participated from 1879 to 1886 in the last five exhibitions of the Impressionist group.

He abandoned his career as a stockbroker, which was declining in 1882, to devote himself entirely to painting. However, the insufficient income from this activity forced him, for a time, to move with his wife and children to Copenhagen, his wife's country.

He doesn't fare well financially, argues with his Danish in-laws, and returns alone first to Rouen, where he paints about forty paintings, and then back to Paris, where he works in ceramics.

In mid-1886, Paul Gauguin goes on a several-month stay to Pont-Aven, which will be crucial in terms of the evolution of his style towards symbolism, as seen in "Four Breton Women."

In November 1887, Gauguin, who has just arrived in Paris, becomes friends with Vincent Van Gogh, especially as they both suffer from depressive episodes. They exchange paintings, make portraits of each other in Montmartre, and endlessly discuss their artist status and social situation.

In 1888, Van Gogh, who has already settled in the city of Arles, is excited to welcome Gauguin, whom he has long requested. He wants the two artists to work together in the same studio, and he even buys two beds in anticipation of his friend's arrival.

Upon arrival, Gauguin paints a portrait of Van Gogh painting his famous sunflowers. Van Gogh is not pleased with this portrait, saying, *"It's me, but gone mad."*

From December 1888, disputes frequently erupt between the two men, with Van Gogh finding Gauguin arrogant and dominating, and especially fearing that he will leave Arles, leaving him alone.

After yet another altercation, Van Gogh enters a psychotic state, as he is accustomed to, and cuts off his ear with a razor.

In early 1891, after living on Rue Delambre in Montparnasse, Gauguin is in a critical financial situation. However, he manages to pay for his passage on a ship bound for Polynesia, to Tahiti, and then to the Marquesas.

He lives with a young Tahitian girl aged 13, while he is 43, which leads to accusations of pedophilia against him.

During this Tahitian stay, he paints 70 canvases, including Two Tahitian Women, or The Breasts with Red Flowers, which is preserved at the Metropolitan Museum of Art in New York (MOMA).

In 1893, Gauguin returns to France, to Paris, moves in with a woman, breaks his tibia during a fight in Concarneau, and becomes lame, thereafter walking with a cane.

He returned alone to Tahiti in 1895, got involved with a 14-year-old girl, drank excessively, painted, became depressed, relieved his pain with morphine, and attempted suicide. In 1897-1898, he painted the now-famous work, Where Do We Come From? What Are We? Where Are We Going?

His health deteriorated, and he was forced to sell paintings to buy morphine and arsenic, both to treat his leg and to try to cure syphilis. He created more paintings for his dealer Vollard, who found them mediocre and refused them.

He later moved to the Marquesas Islands, impregnated a 13-year-old native girl, 39 years his junior, which reignited pedophilia controversies. He quarreled with a policeman, leading to court cases and a stint in prison.

He died in May 1903 at the age of 54, ravaged by syphilis and a festering leg wound, in a simple hut, scorned by the Marquesan and Polynesian communities, who believed he had taken advantage of very young women and provoked local institutions.

Although he died as a tormented artist, Paul Gauguin would posthumously, along with Paul Cézanne, Vincent Van Gogh, and Émile Bernard, become one of the most influential artists for subsequent generations of the 20th century, both for his paintings and the writings and notes he left behind.

One of his quotes is: "*You have long known what I wanted to establish: the right to dare anything.*"

Gradually recognized after his death through retrospectives and certain collectors, he would go on to influence the Fauves (Matisse, Derain, Dufy), the Cubists, the Expressionists, and even Picasso.

Louis Martin, a watchmaker-jeweler, and Zélie Guérin, a lacemaker, who reside in Alençon, already had eight children, four of whom died in infancy, when Zélie gave birth at the age of 40 to a little **Thérèse,** on January 2, 1873.

The family is very pious and charitable, and Thérèse is surrounded by love from her parents and sisters. Unfortunately, her mother is diagnosed with breast cancer and passes away when Thérèse is only four and a half years old. Of course, this is a dreadful tragedy for the little girl, and she will experience great pain over the next ten years.

Her sister Pauline takes over caring for her late mother, and the family moves closer to Louis Martin's brother-in-law, who is a pharmacist in Lisieux, by settling in the Buissonnets, a neighborhood of Lisieux. This pharmacist is a monarchist who advocates for social Catholicism and admires Pope Leo XIII.

Thérèse attended school at the Benedictines for five years, an experience she perceives as a period of sadness, despite being disciplined and a good student.

Then comes the time when her sister Pauline enters the Carmel of Lisieux, and it's a new shock for Thérèse, who is then 10 years old and learns the news by surprise. She falls seriously ill, experiencing hallucinations, anorexia, headaches, rashes, and regression to infantile behavior. Doctors are at a loss for how to bring her out of this state.

Her surroundings pray for her, her sister Pauline sends her comforting letters extolling the joys of life at the Carmel. A statue of the Virgin Mary is placed in her room, and during a communal prayer with her other sisters, Thérèse sees the statue of the Virgin Mary smile at her, and she is instantly cured of her ailment.

Under the questioning of the Carmelites, she feels guilty for having betrayed the Virgin Mary by telling her story; she even thinks she was not really sick, despite the doctors' diagnosis.

Nevertheless, Thérèse makes her first communion in 1884 and feels in complete union with Jesus Christ on that day. A year later, Thérèse discovers the sea in Normandy, in Trouville sur Mer, and in 1886, it is her sister Marie's turn to enter the Carmel. She claims to receive grace on Christmas of that same year, which she will later call the night of her conversion.

Concerned with converting others, especially sinners, Thérèse takes an interest in the fate of a condemned man, Henri Pranzini, a multiple murderer who never repented. She prays for him, asking for a simple sign of conversion, which he will fulfill on the day of his execution by kissing the Cross, although he had refused the assistance of a priest.

Convinced of divine mercy, she believes that God has forgiven Pranzini.

In October 1887, after some deliberations with her father and the pharmacist, who had become her guardian due to Louis Martin's poor health, she is finally allowed to enter the Carmel by her family.

However, she faces resistance from religious authorities who refuse because she is too young and has not yet reached the required age of twenty-one. Undeterred, she takes advantage of a pilgrimage to Rome undertaken by her family on the occasion of Pope Leo XIII's jubilee to present her request directly to the Pope. Although there will still be many obstacles to overcome for her with bishops, canons, and vicars involved in this "combatant's journey," she finally gains admission to the Carmel of Lisieux in April 1888, when she is fifteen years and three months old.

She leads a strictly disciplined, austere, and predominantly contemplative life there. Life is not always easy because the other sisters and superiors are not always tender with Thérèse.

At the age of 65, her beloved father, Louis, suffered from mental disturbances, likely due to cerebral arteriosclerosis, but still managed to witness her taking the habit and entering the novitiate in January 1889. Thérèse chooses her religious name, which will be **"Thérèse of the Child Jesus and of the Holy Face."**

Louis Martin dies in July 1894, and Céline, one of Thérèse's sisters who cared for him, also joins the Carmel. That same year, a national celebration of Joan of Arc and the beginning of the beatification process initiated by Leo XIII are celebrated. This gives Thérèse the opportunity to write two plays about the life of Joan of Arc.

During the year 1896, Thérèse delves deeper into her religious vocation and her profound union with Christ, especially as she is afflicted with tuberculosis and her health deteriorates rapidly. She indicates that her posthumous mission will be to "*give her small voice to souls*" and to "*spend her Heaven doing good on earth.*"

She dies on September 30, 1897, at the age of 24. It is only long after her death that the national and international influence of Thérèse of Lisieux will illuminate the world of Christianity.

The first pilgrims come to pray at her tomb, and some miracles are reported, including the healing of a 4-year-old blind girl at Thérèse's tomb.

On April 29, 1923, she is beatified, and her relics are transferred from the cemetery of Lisieux to the Carmel.

She is canonized on May 17, 1925, by Pope Pius XI, with 50,000 faithful gathered in St. Peter's Square in Rome, at the Vatican.Her name is now Saint Thérèse of Lisieux.

Then, in 1929, the construction of the Basilica of Lisieux begins, which is inaugurated in 1937 and consecrated in 1954. Pope John Paul II visits the basilica on a pilgrimage in 1980.

During World War II, in 1944, Pope Pius XII proclaims Thérèse the secondary patroness of France, on par with Joan of Arc.

Regarding Thérèse, let us quote the words of Bishop Guy Gaucher found on the official website of the Sanctuary of Saint Thérèse of Lisieux: "*The holiness of Thérèse does not rest on extraordinary phenomena. It consists in doing ordinary things in an extraordinary way !*"

WAY NUMBER TWENTY NINE

WAY NUMBER TWENTY-NINE : PUTTING ON A SHOW

On November 16, 1906, **Henri Charrière,** later nicknamed **Papillon,** is born in Saint-Étienne-de-Lugdarès, Ardèche, already having two older sisters at his birth.

Life proves to be tough for young Henri, who doesn't yet know it, unless it's Henri himself who has made his life difficult without realizing it.

At the age of ten, his beloved mother dies from a contagious disease, and he will forever experience this death as the first great injustice towards him.

This event toughens him, especially since his father sends him to boarding school in Crest, Drôme. There, suffering from the loss of his mother, he learns to carve out his place by using his fists, to the point of being expelled from the institution.

His father, wanting to straighten him out, encourages him to join the French Navy, but this born rebel even less accepts military discipline and rebels against it. Soon, he gains a reputation as a hothead, more often punished, placed in solitary confinement, or assigned to toilet duty, rather than serving an active duty position on the aircraft carrier Béarn to which he is assigned.

He signed up for three years with the Navy but only thinks about shortening his commitment to the army before its term expires. After getting a butterfly tattooed on his shoulder during a stop in Calvi, he intentionally crushes his thumb with a stone and manages to be discharged on April 28, 1927, after just two years of service.

After leaving the army, following a brief stint in Ardèche, he settles in Paris with a woman of ill repute, becomes a pimp, and makes a living from petty crime, including safe-cracking. He frequents various penitentiary institutions.

On March 26, 1930, a certain Roland Legrand, a butcher by day and a pimp by night, is shot in the abdomen in the middle of the night. Transported to the hospital, where he dies a few hours later, he has time, in his last breath, to identify the shooter as *"Papillon Roger."* This seals Henri Charrière's fate, better known as *"Papillon thumb-cut."*

The police believe they have the culprit, even though Charrière claims his innocence. His lawyer is confident, and so is Henri, who wears a light blue bow tie. However, he is found guilty, except for premeditation, and sentenced to life forced labor on October 26, 1931, at the age of 25.

Forced labor, it's the hell of French Guiana. Henri swears he won't stay more than two years in the penal colony, and that he will escape. He first heads to the Île de Ré. His fellow inmates don't understand the severity of his sentence, considering it to be a mere peccadillo. It's true that he is among the "hardest of the hard," and he makes a few friends among them. He sets off for French Guiana to Cayenne, in the hold of a ship for an 18-day journey.

The reputation of the Cayenne penal colony is grim as the living conditions of the inmates are miserable. The army manages the administration of the penitentiary. Devil's Island, which had housed Captain Dreyfus, now only has a few hundred inmates.

The convicts are forced to saw wood in the Guyanese forest, this "green hell." No need for locks, as any escape in this hostile environment leads to inevitable death.

However, Papillon succeeds in getting himself hospitalized, which allows him to better prepare an escape from the Saint-Laurent-du-Maroni penal colony.

Papillon finds an accomplice with a small boat who can help him flee via the river, for a price. He succeeds, only injuring himself on the broken glass that lines the walls of the prison.

Papillon and his companions end up on Pigeon Island where the lepers reside. They leave the island on a small sailboat given by the lepers, heading for Colombia and landing in Trinidad in the Caribbean.

An English lawyer hosts them in a huge house with a swimming pool. Henri and his accomplices head back towards Honduras, and near the Colombian coast, they are arrested by a Colombian maritime patrol and incarcerated.

The French trio quickly escape from this prison and find refuge with Colombian Indians, where they take temporary wives. Departing again a year later, they are caught in Santa Marta and incarcerated again under appalling conditions, in dungeons where the rising tide reaches the waist of the prisoners, infested with rats and crabs.

Another escape from this hell, and another failure after a capsizing. Back to Cayenne and an additional two-year sentence on Salvation Island. Henri plans another escape, which again fails due to betrayal, and this time he begins by serving eleven uninterrupted years in the penal colony. He is sent to Devil's Island, in the same cell that was once occupied by Captain Dreyfus.

At over 35 years old, he dreams of a new life and takes the example of Dreyfus who never gave up. He attempts a risky escape by launching himself into the sea, shackled. He succeeds in this new attempt, sailing on a coconut raft for 40 hours and arriving in Guyana.

From the fall of 1967, Papillon benefits from a sentence prescription, returning to France after several decades in exile, and during the following six months, Henri Charrière compulsively writes the story of his life in 600 pages.

The book Papillon is published by the editor Robert Laffont in 1969, with Henri Charrière then being 63 years old. His memoirs sell millions of copies, with over 13 million copies sold worldwide. Overnight, Charrière becomes a star. He is pardoned in 1970 by President Georges Pompidou.

Although the publisher Laffont claims to have verified Papillon's story before publication, serious doubts about its truthfulness arise, particularly based on the statements of Charrière's former fellow inmates. Publisher Gérard de Villiers takes it upon himself to verify the facts and finds that most of them are either embellished, entirely fabricated, or happened to other inmates rather than Charrière.

Charrière publishes a sequel to his story in 1972, in a book titled Banco, and in 1973, a film adaptation enters theaters, with Franklin Schaffner's film Papillon, starring Steve McQueen as Papillon and Dustin Hoffman.

Henri Charrière dies at the age of 67 from throat cancer, in Madrid, Spain.

Jacques Mayol, nicknamed **Dolphin Man**, committed suicide by hanging in his villa on the island of Elba at the age of 74 because he no longer believed in anything and suffered from depression.

He was born in Shanghai on April 1, 1927, a day when people attach a fish to their back for April Fools' Day, and this nod of fate from the hanging that takes his breath away illustrates the two parentheses that frame his life, entirely dedicated to the sea and deep free diving.

His father is an architect and works in the French concession of the city. The family often travels to Japan, and from the age of six, Jacques and his brother Pierre become passionate about the Ama, these breath-holding female divers, who, equipped with just a wicker basket, gather shells, sea urchins, and crustaceans to make a living.

It is also the time when he first discovers dolphins, particularly around the caves of Karatsu.

In 1939, Jacques and his family settled in Marseille, and during the Second World War, he had plenty of time to make frequent dives along the coast to fish with makeshift equipment.

It is there, in the Calanques, that he becomes friends with Albert Falco, who would later become the associate of Commander Cousteau in his numerous maritime adventures.

Jacques isn't cut out for studies, and he quickly travels the world, pursuing his three greatest passions : the road, the sea, and women.

During a stay in Miami, where he settles with a Danish woman he married, he finds a job that suits him in 1955, namely as a diver to clean the aquariums at Seaquarium. This activity allows him to make a friend : a female dolphin named Clown, who would later become the mother of Flipper the dolphin in a TV series. He learns some free diving behaviors from her.

Later, in 1986, he writes Homo Delphinus, in which he explains how Clown taught him *"to become aquatic, to let go, to surrender to the flow of water, to the flow of life."*

The rest is a series of romantic adventures and a cascade of different jobs ranging from chauffeur to Hollywood stars, where he notably drives Zsa Zsa Gabor and a mistress of Frank Sinatra and Sean Connery, to lobster fishermen, to treasure hunters in the Bahamas, or even a diver in restaurants !

His multiple professional and romantic adventures, along with his international wandering, allow him to form friendships across the board and develop exceptional adaptability skills, as his brother Pierre Mayol would write in an autobiographical book, Mayol, the Dolphin Man.

Until the early 1960s, the scientific community and divers believed it was impossible to dive deeper than 50 meters on a single breath, without having one's rib cage reduced to mush.

It was the Italian Enzo Maiorca who first had the courage to break through this kind of sound barrier in free diving, on August 15, 1961, off the coast of Syracuse, successfully diving to a depth of 51 meters.

From that time on, Jacques Mayol and Enzo Maiorca engaged in a fierce competition in the field of free diving, breaking records one after another. In 1966, Mayol dethrones Maiorca by achieving a dive to 61 meters in the Bahamas.

In 1972, Maiorca reaches 80 meters, a record that Mayol surpasses in November 1976 by becoming the first free-diver to exceed 100 meters. Jacques Mayol used techniques inspired by yoga to accomplish his feats and significantly slow down his heart rate while diving.

However, the year before, Jacques Mayol experiences a horrifying tragedy : his German girlfriend, Gerda, is attacked with a knife and killed in Florida by a drug addict in a supermarket. Mayol never recovers from this and develops melancholy for the rest of his life following this tragic event.

It is in 1983, in Marseille, that Jacques Mayol meets the director Luc Besson. The latter has the project of making a film about the rivalry between Enzo Maiorca and Jacques Mayol and their determination to push the limits of their passion for deep free diving ever further. That same year, Mayol dives to 105 meters.

Jacques Mayol participates in the film's screenplay, without informing Maiorca. The latter will later say : *"I especially didn't appreciate that Jacques, who participated in the screenplay, never mentioned it to me. I felt betrayed."*

The film, titled The Big Blue, is a rather loose interpretation of the real story of the two divers. It is presented as the opening film at the Cannes Film Festival in 1988, where it receives a very mixed reception. It is even booed by part of the audience. Jacques Mayol is then 61 years old, and his fame will be reinforced by the film, as everyone knows that the film tells his story.

Despite this unpromising start, The Big Blue proves to be one of the most profitable French films of all time, with over 9 million spectators in France alone. The film receives six nominations at the Cesar Awards and wins the Cesar for Best Music, composed by Éric Serra, and Best Sound. The success is less pronounced in the rest of Europe and the United States.

In France, the success of the film gives Jacques Mayol the feeling of being deprived of his life and increases his sense of loneliness. This lasting melancholy will lead him to end his life about a decade later.

WAY NUMBER THIRTY

WAY NUMBER THIRTY: WRITING A BOOK ON WAYS TO BECOME FAMOUS LATER IN LIFE OR FINDING THE THIRTY-FIRST WAY

The author of this book, aged 72, having remained anonymous until now, this thirtieth way to achieve a certain form of notoriety later in life will be validated if this book experiences success, other than pure esteem and self-satisfaction.

I didn't write this book just to test this thirtieth method, but mainly because I remain fascinated by the fact that so many elderly people have taken the twenty-nine others, demonstrated unsuspected resources and dismantled many prejudices about age.

The Japanese life philosophy of **Ikigai,** born on the island of Okinawa, which boasts many centenarians, is a philosophy based on the idea of feeling happy to exist, no matter what happens and when.

To find your Ikigai, the method consists first in determining what you love to do, your passions, and your main interests. Then, identify your talents and what you can do, especially something worthwhile in. Then, reflect on what others need and how you could give meaning to your life to bring them something.

Finally, why not combine the useful with the pleasant by completing the last part of this philosophy, namely, how to monetize this talent, which is our passion, and which provides a service to others.

Many of the characters mentioned in this book have found their Ikigai, consciously or unconsciously, have discovered why their life was worth living, regardless of age, and have never thought that the latter constituted a limit beyond which your ticket was no longer valid.

It now falls to all those who have made the effort to read this book so far, and beyond themselves, to invent or discover the thirty-first way, the one that I have not previously listed, and which will make them known beyond retirement age.

I am certain that there is enough imagination, new ideas, unsuspected energy, hidden and still unrevealed talents, throughout the vast world, to be surprised once again by new ways of achieving national or international notoriety at an age when it is more customary to be discreet.

PUNCH LINE

One of the teachings of this book is that every human being possesses three ages: the official age, that of our birth certificate and civil status. That one, we cannot hide it; we can only assume it, whether well or poorly, and we know that it adds one more year with each of our birthdays.

This official age, which we cannot change, bothers some people to the point that they decide to disguise it on social media or in conversations. For those, it is recommended not to wish them a happy birthday when the clock has already struck many times, as this cursed day gives them no desire to uncork champagne or blow out candles numbered with only two digits to avoid overloading a cake that could not bear the real number.

Our second age is the one we have in our heads. Most often, it shaves off several years, or even decades, from our official age. *"We are always twenty years old when we love,"* as Quebecois singer **Jean-Pierre Ferland** wrote in 1975. And then our living conditions and health have improved so much that we are still very young at 50. The retirement age is increasing, allowing us to remain active longer.

Some of us feel more mature and want to skip the stages of life. This is often the case with teenagers, who feel older than they are, and want to act like adults.

Conversely the "boomerang generation" want to return to their teenage years, to stay under the protective parental umbrella, because they no longer accept their adult status in their minds.

Some people age themselves in their heads because it gives them more confidence, maturity, or authority. We see that in the corporate world, where young managers try to mimic their older boss.

In any case, as psychiatrist and geriatrician **Olivier de Ladoucette** says: *"We are not only as old as our arteries, but we are also as old as our desires."* The success of dating apps for seniors and their intensive use of social networks clearly demonstrates this.

The third age, if I may say so, is the one that people around you lend you. You can appear younger or older than your official age, depending on your physical condition, morale and mindset, addictions, activities, or many other criteria.

The success of cosmetic surgery, despite its often-exorbitant cost, dietary supplements, sports or wellness clubs, thalassotherapy or massage institutes, meditation and relaxation seminars, tanning booths, dental or hair implants, skin cosmetics, and other means, clearly show this somewhat desperate quest for youthful appearance.

Ultimately, all this matters little if we adhere to the excellent phrase of **Oscar Wilde**: *"Beauty is in the eye of the beholder."*

However, we also know that some young people already seem old, entrenched in principles, habits, outdated reflections, or narrow-mindedness. Being twenty years old and spending evenings in slippers watching Netflix series while drinking chamomile tea, yes, that exists, and the "boring" generation generates as many "young old" as the midlife crisis generates "old beauties."

Where a problem may arise is when the gap between the age in your head and the age attributed to you becomes too significant, as then, ridicule, or even grotesqueness, may emerge.

This situation can lead fifty-year-old mothers to want to dress up, put on makeup, and go out to the same places as their twenty-year-old daughters. Sometimes even to seduce and sleep with their daughters' boyfriends. Older gentlemen in their sixties or older may want to erase the 40 years that separate them from the young women or men they covet and end up joining "sugar daddy" sites.

Of course, there is no normality in romantic relationships, if one does not break the law, and there should not be inappropriate judgment on these situations. Yet, we know well that *"what will people say?"* builds around them because there is an eternal propensity among humans in the realm of love to find it easier to mock an exception rather than rejoice in it in the name of individual freedom for each.

We can see that nowadays; official age is not an obstacle but just a number. And as **Friedrich Nietzsche** wrote in The Gay Science: *"Rust is also necessary: being sharp is not enough! Otherwise, people will always say of you: he is too young!"*

In France, the famous singer **Hughes Aufray**, 94 years old, recently married with Murielle, 45 years younger was asked about his energy and longevity. He said, *" the secret is that I don't have any secret. I t would be too easy to tell you it's this or that. It's a set of things, an art of living."*

Micheline Presle, recently deceased as the doyenne of French cinema at the age of 102, used to say: *"I don't like to say my age because it would give it importance."*

BIOGRAPHICAL SOURCES

1. Louise Bourgeois: Museum of Modern Art MoMA - New York; The Solomon R. Guggenheim - New York; Xavier Hufkens

2. Katsushika Hokusai: Katsushika Hokusai.org; Britannica; The Metropolitan Museum of Art MoMA -New York; British Museum.

3. Yayoi Kusama: Yayoi Kusama Official Site; www.tate.org.uk; Artnet; Britannica; MoMA.

4. Jorge Mario Bergoglio: La Croix; The Holy See (https://m.vatican.va), Britannica.

5. Rut Larsson: Guiness World Records; New York Post (June 15, 2022).

6. Yūichiro Miura: Guiness World Records, Wikipedia; Smithsonian Magazine; The Japan News (31 août 2023).

7. Fauna Singh: Olympics (https://olympics.com), BBC; Wikipedia.

8. Olga Kotelko: olgakotelko.com; National Institutes of Health (https://www.ncbi.nlm.nih.go).

9. Julia Welles Hawkins: Gerontology Wiki (https://gerontology.fandom.com/wiki/Julia_Hawkins); Guideposts(https://guideposts.org).

10. Pierre Agostini: NobelPrize.org; CEA (https://www.cea.fr);Wikipedia

11. Luc Montagnier: NobelPrize.org; The Lancet (https://thelancet.com); Institut Pasteur (https://www.pasteur.fr).

12. Louis Pasteur: Institut Pasteur (https://www.pasteur.fr); Britannica.

13. Vernon Lomax Smith: NobelPrize.org; Encyclopedia.com

14. Peter W. Higgs: NobelPrize.org; The Guardian (https://www.theguardian.com)Physics World (https://physicsworld.com); The World Economic Forum (https://wefo. rum.org).

15. John Goodwin: Virgin Galactic (https://www.virgingalactic.com); Olympics (https://olympics.com); Wikipedia.

16. Wally Funk: Guiness World Records; wallyfly.com (https://wallyfly.com); NASA (https://historycollection.jsc.nasa.gov).

17. Helen Van Winkle: Linkedin; Wikipedia; CNN (https://money.cnn.com).

18. Studio Danielle: Le Temps (https://www.letemps.ch); Instagram; X; FamousBirthdays (https://fr.famousbirthdays.com).

19. Shirley Curry: YouTube; Wikipedia; The New York Times (https://www.nytimes.com)

20. Jeanne-Marie Le Calvé dit "La Mère Denis": Radio France (https://www.radiofrance.fr);Geneastar(https://www.geneastar.org; Graines de Robert (https://graines-de-robert.e-monsite.com)

21. Germaine Soleil: France 3 Régions (https://france3-regions.francetvinfo.fr); Histoires radiophoniques (https://radios.peuleux.eu); ina.fr (https://www.ina.fr).

22. Marguerite Yourcenar: Académie française (https://www.academie-francaise.fr); Musée Marguerite Yourcenar (https://www.museeyourcenar.fr); Radio France (https://www.radiofrance.fr); Site Gallimard (https://www.gallimard.fr).

23. Annie Ernaux: Annie-Ernaux.org (https://www.annie-ernaux.org); NobelPrize.org; Britannica; Wikipédia.

24. Katherine Anne Porter: Britannica; PBS (www.pbs.org); Wikipedia; University of Maryland.

25. Harland David Sanders: KFC UK (https://www.kfc.co.uk); Britannica; University of Houston (https://uh.edu); Biography (https://www.biography.com).

26. Didier Lombard: Le Monde (https://www.lemonde.fr); The World Economic Forum; Les Annales des Mines (https://www.annales.org); L'Usine Nouvelle (https://www.usinenouvelle.com); France Info; Courrier international (https://www.courrierinternational.com).

27. Warren Buffet: Forbes (https://www.forbes.com); Harvard Business Review (https://hbr.org); Berkshire Hathaway; CNBC, Britannica.

28. Didier Raoult: IHU-Méditerranée Infection; France Info; Radio France; Challenges (https://www.challenges.fr); Le Monde.

29. Gaston Dominici: INA (https://www.ina.fr); Historia; Radio France; Le Monde, Wikipedia.

30. Bernard Madoff: Britannica; United States Department of Justice; Investopedia (https://www.investopedia.com); Wikipedia.

31. Harvey Weinstein: BBC (https://www.bbc.com); The New York Times; Time Magazine; Reuters

(https://www.reuters.com); ABC News (https://abc-news.go.com)

32. Leonid Ilitch Brejnev: History.com (https://www.history.com); Encyclopedia of Ukraine (https://www.encyclopediaofukraine.com); Wikipedia; Britannica.

33. Deng Xiaoping: People's Daily Online (http://en.people.cn/data/people/dengxiaoping.shtml); Chineseposters.net; Biography (https://www.biography.com); Association for Asian Studies.

34. Rolihlahla Mandela: Nelson Mandela Foundation (https://www.nelsonmandela.org/biography); NobelPrize.org; Britannica.

35. Golda Meir: Jewish Women's Archive (https://jwa.org/encyclopedia/article/meir-golda); National Geographic; History.com.

36. Joe Biden: The White House (https://www.whitehouse.gov); Wikipédia; National Archives (https://obamawhitehouse.gov).

37. Comte de Saint Germain/Richard Chanfray: Savoirs d'Histoire (https://savoirsdhistoire.wordpress.com); Musica et Memoria (http://www.musimem.com); Wikipédia; Dalida site Officiel (https://dalida.com); chemeurope.com.

38. Baba Vanga: Sky History TV Channel; Wikipédia.

39. Philippe Aries: philippe-aries.histoweb.net; Encyclopedia.com; Larousse.

40. Jean de Joinville: Encyclopedia Universalis (https://www.universalis.fr); france-pittoresque.com

41. Claude Bloch: Convoi 77 (https://convoi77.org); Mémorial de la Shoah (https://www.memorialdelashoah.org).

42. Sunna Tsuboi: Wikipédia; The New York Times; Asahi Shinbun (https://www.asahi.com).

43. Léon Gautier: Ministère des Armées (https://www.defense.gouv.fr); D-Day Overlord (https://www.dday-over-

lord.com); Les services de l'État dans le Calvados (https://www.calvados.gouv.fr).

44. Elizabeth Gladys Dean, dite Millvina: Encyclopedia Titanica (https://www.encyclopedia-titanica.org); Biography (https://www.biography.com); Wikipédia.

45. Lazare Ponticelli: Musée de l'histoire de l'immigration (https://www.histoire-immigration.fr); Légion Étrangère (https://www.legion-etrangere.com); Encyclopaedia Universalis.

46. Carlos Soria Fontán: BBVA (https://www.bbva.com); Wikipédia; BBC (https://www.bbc.com).

47. Georges Clemenceau: Musée Clemenceau (https://musee-clemenceau.fr); Sénat (https://www.senat.fr); Académie française (https://www.academie-francaise.fr).

48. Donald John Trump: Association Donald John Trump: National Archives (https://trumpwhitehouse.archives.gov); The Trump Organization (https://www.trump.com); White House Historical (https://www.whitehousehistory.org).

49. Jean-Luc Mélenchon: Melenchon.fr; La France Insoumise (https://lafranceinsoumise.fr); Assemblée Nationale (https://www.assemblee-nationale.fr).

50. Jean-Marie Le Pen: Site Officiel (http://www.jean-marielepen.com); Assemblée Nationale (https://www.assemblee-nationale.fr); Ina (https://www.ina.fr).

51. Paul Richard Alexander: The New York Times; BBC (https://www.bbc.com); Dallas News (https://www.dallasnews.com).

52. Charly Bancarel: Olympics (https://olympics.com); Wikipédia.

53. Ana del Valle: Radio France (https://www.radiofrance.fr); Wikipédia.

54. James Hiram Bedford: Cryonics Archive (https://www.cryonicsarchive.org); The New York Times; SFGATE (https://www.sfgate.com).

55. Jean-Pierre Adams : OGC Nice (https://www.ogcnice.com); Fédération Française de Football (https://www.fff.fr); Wikipédia.

56. Cornelia Ras: Reuters (https://www.reuters.com); Gerontology Wiki (https://gerontology.fandom.com).

57. Paul von Hindenburg: Fondation Charles de Gaulle (https://www.charles-de-gaulle.org); Seconde-Guerre.com; Geo (https://www.geo.fr).

58. Cochise: Encyclopaedia Universalis (https://www.universalis.fr); Medarus.org; SouthernArizonaGuide.com.

59. Henri Philippe Pétain: Chemins de Mémoire (https://www.cheminsdememoire.gouv.fr); Académie Française; Géo.fr; L'Histoire (https://www.lhistoire.fr).

60. Arthur Schopenhauer: Philosophie Magazine (https://www.philomag.com); Radio France; Larousse; Schopenhauer.fr.

61. Edgar Morin: Philosophie Magazine; Institut Mémoires de l'édition contemporaine (https://www.imec-archives.com); Radio France; Wikipédia.

62. Sigmund Freud: Philosophie Magazine; Encyclopaedia Universalis; Radio France; Larousse; Wikipédia.

63. Iris Apfel: Vogue France; MODART International (https://wwwmodart-paris.com); Fashion Network; Courrier International; Vanity Fair.

64. Jacques Henri Lartigue: Donation Lartigue (https://www.lartigue.org); Musée de la Photographie Charles Nègre; INA (https://www.ina.fr); Wikipédia.

65. Rose Victoria Repetto: Repetto (https://repetto.com/pages/univers-repetto-histoire); Mondepotvente.com; Wikipédia.

66. Judith Olivia Dench: Club James Bond (https://james-bond007.net); Purepeople (https://www.purepeople.com); Wikipédia.Youn Yuh-Jung: Academy of Motion Picture Arts and Sciences; The Korea Herald; Wikipédia.

67. Youn Yuh-Jung: Academy of Motion Picture Arts and Sciences; The Korea Herald; Wikipédia.

68. Ridley Scott: Larousse; Institut Lumière (https://www.institut-lumiere.org); Wikipédia; Britannica.

69. Ann Roth: Costume Designers Guild (https://www.costumedesignersguild.com); The New York Times; Wikipédia.

70. Ramjit Raghav: Daily Mail; India Today; World Record Academy; Wikipédia.

71. Omkari Panwar: World Record Academy; London Evening Standard; WordPress.com; Wikipédia.

72. Robert De Niro: Vanity Fair; Gala (https://www.gala.fr); Dailymotion.

73. Al Pacino: Gala; Purepeople; Voici (https://www.voici.fr

74. Anthony Quinn: Wikipédia.

75. Ninon de Lenclos : Histoire pour Tous (https://www.histoire-pou-tous.fr); Carnet d'Histoire (https://carnet-dhistoire.fr); Larousse.

76. Massimo Gargia: YouTube; Gala; Voici; Le Journal des Femmes.

77. Zsa Zsa Gabor: Wikipédia; Gala; Purepeople; Hollywood Walk of Fame (https://walkoffame.com).

78. Richard Lemieuvre/Richard Allan : Wikipédia; Allo Ciné; Academic (https://fr-academic.com).

79. Shigeo Tokuda: VOI.ID (https://voi.id/framp/29461); Ici-Japon; Academic; Wikipédia.

80. Dominique Aderweireld, dit Dodo la Saumure: Wikipédia; Mouvement du Nid; Le Monde; RTBF; France Info.

81. Dennis Hof: Las Vegas Sun; The New York Times; The Nevada Independent (https://thenevadaindependent.com); Wikipédia.

82. Mère Teresa: Secrétariat General du Synode des Évêques (http://secretariat.synod.va/content.html); Vatican News (http://www.vaticannews.cn/fr); Le Jour du Seigneur (https://www.lejourduseigneur.com); France Catholique.

83. Madeleine Cinquin dite Soeur Emmanuelle : Le Pèlerin (https://www.lepelerin.com); La Grande Chancellerie (https://www.legiondhonneur.fr); Le Jour du Seigneur; Encyclopedia Universalis.

84. Mohandas Karamchand Gandhi: Larousse; Wikipédia; Radio France; La Croix.

85. Jeanne Louise Calment : INA (https://www.ina.fr); Wikipédia; France Info; Archives Départementales des Bouches du Rhone.

86. Jiroemon Kimura: Wikipédia; The Famous People (https://www.thefamouspeople.com); The Guardian (https://www.theguardian.com).

87. Theodore Struyck: The Palm Beach Post (https://www.palmbeachpost.com); The US Sun (https://www.the-sun.com).

88. Gloria Mackenzie: The Mirror (https://www.mirror.c0.uk); CNBC (https://www.cnbc.com).

89. Dennis Banfield: The Mirror; The Sun (https://www.the-sun.co.uk).

90. Francis Charles Chichester : Britannica ; Rolex (https://www.rolex.org); La Voile (http://www.lavoile.com); Royal Museums Greenwich (https://www.rmg.co.uk).

91. Alejandra Rodriguez: Hindustan Times (https://www.hindustantimes.com); People (https://people.com); The Times of India (https://timesofindi.indiatimes.com).

92. René Angélil: Purepeople (https://www.purepeople.com); Ordre National du Quebec (https://www.ordre-na-

tional.gouv.qc.ca); The Canadian Encyclopedia (https://www.thecanadianencyclopedia.ca).

93. Thomas Wayne Markle: Wikipédia; The Mirror; Purepeople; The Sun; Point de Vue (https://www.pointdevue.fr).

94. Jamie Parnell Spears: Wikipédia; Forbes France; Daily Mail; Radio France.

95. Mohamed Al-Fayed: Purepeople (https://www.purepeople.com); Arab News; Wikipédia (https://fr.wikipedia.org); France Info; Dailymotion.

96. Paul Cézanne: Atelier de Cézanne (https://www.cezanne-en-provence.com); Grand Palais (https://www.grandpalais.fr); Impressioniste.net (http://www.impressioniste.net); Société Cézanne (https://www.societe-cezanne.fr).

97. Paul Gauguin: Beaux Arts (https://www.beauxarts.com); Impressioniste.net; Carré d'Artistes (https://www.carredartistes.com); Grand Palais.

98. Thérèse de l'Enfant Jésus et de la Sainte Face: Sanctuaire de Lisieux (https://www.therese-de-lisieux.catholique.fr); Archives du Carmel de Lisieux (https://archives.carmeldelisieux.fr); Secrétariat du Synode du Vatican (http://secretariat.synod.va).

99. Henri Charrière : papillon-charriere.com ; Wikipedia ; Le Point ; Vanity Fair (https://www.vanityfair.fr).

100. Jacques Mayol: France Info; Wikipédia; Le Temps (https://www.letemps.ch); France Apnée (https://www.franceapnee.com); CinéSérie (https://www.cineserie.com).